Selected Poems

EDWIN MORGAN

Selected Poems

To Sheila
with best wishes
Edwin Morgan

CARCANET

First published in 1985 by
Carcanet Press Limited
208-212 Corn Exchange Buildings
Manchester M4 3BQ

British Library Cataloguing in Publication Data
Morgan, Edwin
  Selected poems.
  I. Title
  821'.914   PR6063.O69

ISBN 0-85635-596-8

The publisher acknowledges the financial assistance
of the Arts Council of Great Britain.

Typeset by Bryan Williamson, Swinton, Berwickshire
Printed in England by SRP Ltd, Exeter

Contents

Acknowledgements

Previously uncollected poems in this selection were first published in *Saltire Review, Poor.Old.Tired.Horse, Broadsheet, Words Broadsheet, New Edinburgh Review, Literary Review, Poetry Review, Strata, The Poet's Voice, Ambit,* and *Labrys,* to whose editors grateful acknowledgement is due.

The idea of the sequence of 26 poems entitled 'An Alphabet of Goddesses' was first formulated following a visit I made in September 1982 to an exhibition of pastel drawings by Ms Pat Douthwaite, entitled 'Worshipped Women: An Alphabet of Greek Goddesses', at the 369 Gallery in Edinburgh. I wish to acknowledge the contribution made by Ms Douthwaite's drawings and by her accompanying notes to the pictures by which this sequence of poems was inspired and I am grateful for her permission to publish the poems. I am grateful also to have the permission of Mr Robert Graves, who wrote the introduction to the exhibition catalogue.

Stanzas of the Jeopardy

It may be at midday, limousines in cities, the groaning
Derrick and hissing hawser alive at dockyards,
Liners crawling with heat-baked decks, their élite
Drinking languid above the hounded turbines,
Doorways and crossroads thronged with a hundred rendezvous,
Planes low over spire and cupola with screaming
Jet-streams or soaring inaudible in disembodied calm,
Plough-teams on headlands in the sweat of noon, the warm
Earth up-ruffled swarming for crow and gull,
Boys whistling and calling at play in the sea-caves,
Cables humming, telephonists sighing, sirens
Wailing twelve from workshop and factory, tar
Bubbling in the skin of the street, shopfronts shimmering,
In Times Square, Leicester Square, Red Square — that the roar,
    the labour,
The onset and the heat, the engine and the flurry and the errand,
The plane and the phone and the plough and the farm, the farmer
And the stoker and the airman and the docker and the shopper
    and the boy
Shall all be called to a halt:
In the middle of the day, and in the twinkling of an eye.

It could be at midnight, braziers smouldering on wharves,
Watchmen dozing by the tar-boiler's hulk, warehouses
Planted gloomily in bloodless night-idleness,
Desolate siding and shed and circuit littered
With the truck and trash marooned by ebbing daytime,
Astronomers at their mirrors in zodiacal quiet, dancers
Swept through the rosy fantasy of muted waltzes,
Children speaking to the wind and stars in dream,
Great lakes of darkness mountain-locked and moonless
Breaking to the meagre splash of angler's oar,
Badger and hedgehog rooting among the beech-mast, gardens
Swirling with scents disessenced by the dawn,
Lovers lying in the dunes of summer, swimmers
Flashing like sudden fire in the bay — that the play,

The sleep and the pleasure, the tryst, the glow, the tranquillity,
The water and the silence, the fragrance, the vigil, and the kiss,
The fishermen and the slumberers and the whisperers and the
    creatures of the wood
Shall craze to an intolerable blast
And hear at midnight the very end of the world.

"Shall the trumpet sound before the suns have cooled?
Shall there not be portents of blood, sea-beds laid bare,
Concrete and girder like matchwood in earthquake and whirl-
    wind?
Shall we not see the angels, or the creeping icecap, or the moon
Falling, or the wandering star, feel veins boiling
Or fingers freezing or the wind thickening with wings?"
The earth may spin beyond apocalypse;
Long before entropy the worlds may stop.
The heart praises its own intentions, while the moment,
The neighbour, the need, the face of love and the tears
Have passed unseized, as some day they will pass
Beyond all action, beyond despair and redemption,
When matter has uttered its last sound, when the eye
That roved around the universe goes blind, when lips
To lips are numb, when space is rolled away
And time is torn from its rings, and the door of life
Flies open on unimaginable things —
At noon, at midnight, or at no time,
As you receive these verses, O Corinthians.

Verses for a Christmas Card

    This endyir starnacht blach and klar
    As I on Cathkin-fells held fahr
    A snaepuss fusspall showerdown
    With nezhny smirl and whirlcome rown
    Upon my pollbare underlift,

And smazzled all my gays with srift:
Faroer fieldswhide frosbloom strayfling,
Froral brookrims hoartrack glassling,
Allairbelue beauheaven ablove
Avlanchbloomfondshowed brrumalljove.

O angellighthoused harbourmoon,
Glazegulfgalaxeval governoon,
Jovegal allcapellar jupiterror
And you brighdsun of venusacre,
Respour this leidyear Phoenixmas
With starphire and restorying dazz
Bejeweleavening cinderill
To liftlike pace and goodquadrille.
All men reguard, from grace our fere,
And sun on us to kind and chere.

Message Clear

```
      am              i
                                  if
    i am                        he
        he r        o
        h     ur    t
        the re          and
        he     re     and
        he re
      a               n   d
        the r              e
    i am    r                    ife
                 i  n
             s      ion and
    i                    d     i e
      am   e res   ect
      am   e res   ection
                     o              f
        the                      life
                     o              f
      m    e          n
             sur e
        the              d     i e
    i          s
             s    e t     and
    i am the    sur        d
      a    t    res    t
                     o          life
    i am  he r                    e
    i a          ct
    i        r  u      n
    i  m   e  e      t
    i              t              i e
    i          s    t     and
    i am th          o       th
    i am    r              a
    i am the   su       n
    i am the    s        on
    i am the   e    rect on      e if
    i am     re         n    t
    i am       s        a          fe
    i am       s    e   n    t
    i    he e              d
    i    t e  s     t
    i        re           a d
      a    th re           a d
      a        s    t on       e
      a    t   re           a d
      a    th r      on         e
    i         resurrect
                         a          life
    i am              i  n          life
    i am      resurrection
    i am the resurrection and
    i am
    i am the resurrection and the life
```

12

Dialeck Piece

```
                i
a    m
        m    ick          th    e
    d  i      ck
        i                    h ave
        me
        m              a t      e
                     in
        me              a th
a       .n
a d i       ck  i          e
    da    n      in  th    e
              n ick
        me
    da
a d  m    i    r in  th a e
    da m  n              t
    d  i      icker in
        m    ic e      a t
        a    n
a            cker
a d i       c e      thra
a daimen icker in a thrave
```

Strawberry Fields Forever

my blackie

                                        smirr

losing

                        foxpaw

        patter

                            your hazel

            whistle

                    dewdrop

        kneedeep

                unreal

                    the fields we

Archives

```
generation upon
generation upon
generation upon
generation upon
generation upon
generation upon
generation upon
generation upon
generation upon
generation upon
generation upon
generation upon
generation upon
generation upon
generation upon
generation upon
generation upon
generation upon
generation upon
g neration upon
g neration up  n
g nerat on up  n
g nerat  n up  n
g nerat  n  p  n
g   erat  n  p  n
g   era   n  p  n
g   era   n      n
g   er    n      n
g    r    n      n
g         n      n
g         n
g
```

Astrodome

"As real grass withers in the Astrodome
[at Houston, Texas] it has been
replaced by Astrograss."
(news item)

all is not grass that astrograss
that astrograss is not all grass
that grass is not all astrograss
astrograss is not all that grass
is that astrograss not all glass
not all astrograss is that glass
all that glass is not astrograss
that is not all astrograss glass
that glass is not all fibreglass
not all that fibreglass is glass
fibreglass is not all that glass
is that not all fibreglass glass
that fibreglass is not all grass
glass is not all that fibreglass
is all astrograss not that glass
all is not grass that fibregrass

Starryveldt

starryveldt
  slave
southvenus
  serve
SHARPEVILLE
  shove
shriekvolley
  swerve
shootvillage
  save
spoorvengeance
  stave
spadevoice
  starve
strikevault
  strive
subvert
  starve
smashverwoerd
  strive
scattervoortrekker
  starve
spadevow
  strive
sunvast
  starve
survive
  strive
SO:VAEVICTIS

Siesta of a Hungarian Snake

s sz sz SZ sz SZ sz ZS zs ZS zs zs z

The Computer's First Christmas Card

```
j o l l y m e r r y
h o l l y b e r r y
j o l l y b e r r y
m e r r y h o l l y
h a p p y j o l l y
j o l l y j e l l y
j e l l y b e l l y
b e l l y m e r r y
h o l l y h e p p y
j o l l y M o l l y
m a r r y J e r r y
m e r r y H a r r y
h o p p y B a r r y
h e p p y J a r r y
b o p p y h e p p y
b e r r y j o r r y
j o r r y j o l l y
m o p p y j e l l y
M o l l y m e r r y
J e r r y j o l l y
b e l l y b o p p y
j o r r y h o p p y
h o l l y m o p p y
B a r r y m e r r y
J a r r y h a p p y
h a p p y b o p p y
b o p p y j o l l y
j o l l y m e r r y
m e r r y m e r r y
m e r r y m e r r y
m e r r y C h r i s
a m m e r r y a s a
C h r i s m e r r y
a s M E R R Y C H R
Y S A N T H E M U M
```

Opening the Cage

14 variations on 14 words

I have nothing to say and I am saying it and that is poetry.
John Cage

I have to say poetry and is that nothing and am I saying it
I am and I have poetry to say and is that nothing saying it
I am nothing and I have poetry to say and that is saying it
I that am saying poetry have nothing and it is I and to say
And I say that I am to have poetry and saying it is nothing
I am poetry and nothing and saying it is to say that I have
To have nothing is poetry and I am saying that and I say it
Poetry is saying I have nothing and I am to say that and it
Saying nothing I am poetry and I have to say that and it is
It is and I am and I have poetry saying say that to nothing
It is saying poetry to nothing and I say I have and am that
Poetry is saying I have it and I am nothing and to say that
And that nothing is poetry I am saying and I have to say it
Saying poetry is nothing and to that I say I am and have it

Chinese Cat

```
p  m  r  k  g  n  i  a  o  u
p  m  r  k  g  n  i  a  o
p  m  r  k  n  i  a  o
p  m  r  n  i  a  o
p  m  r  i  a  o
p  m  i  a  o
m  i  a  o
m  a  o
```

19

Clydesdale

go
    fetlocksnow
           go
             gullfurrow
                  go

go
    brassglow
          go
           sweatflow
               go

go
    plodknow
          go
           clodshow
               go

go
    leatherbelow
          go
           potatothrow
                 go

go
    growfellow
          go
           crowfollow
               go

go
    Balerno
          go
           Palermo
              whoa

Centaur

i am, horse
unhorse, me
i am, horse
unhorse, me
i am, horse
unhorse, me
i am, horse
unhorse, me
i am, horse
unhorse, me
i am, horse
unhorse, me
i am, horse
unhorse, me
i am horse:
unhorse me!

The Death of Marilyn Monroe

What innocence? Whose guilt? What eyes? Whose breast?
Crumpled orphan, nembutal bed,
white hearse, Los Angeles,
DiMaggio! Los Angeles! Miller! Los Angeles! America!
That Death should seem the only protector —
That all arms should have faded, and the great cameras and lights
    become an inquisition and a torment —
That the many acquaintances, the autograph-hunters, the
    inflexible directors, the drive-in admirers should become
    a blur of incomprehension and pain —
That lonely Uncertainty should limp up, grinning, with
    bewildering barbiturates, and watch her undress and lie
    down and in her anguish
call for him! call for him to strengthen her with what could only
    dissolve her! A method
of dying, we are shaken, we see it. Strasberg!
Los Angeles! Olivier! Los Angeles! Others die
and yet by this death we are a little shaken, we feel it,
America.
Let no one say communication is a cantword.
They had to lift her hand from the bedside telephone.
But what she had not been able to say
perhaps she had said. "All I had was my life.
I have no regrets, because if I made
any mistakes, I was responsible.
There is now — and there is the future.
What has happened is behind. So
it follows you around? So what?" — This
to a friend, ten days before.
And so she was responsible.
And if she was not responsible, not wholly responsible, Los
    Angeles? Los Angeles? Will it follow you around? Will the
    slow white hearse of the child of America follow you around?

The White Rhinoceros

'Rare over most of its former range'
Webster's Third New International Dictionary

The white rhinoceros was eating phosphorus!
I came up and I shouted Oh no! No! No! —
you'll be extinct in two years! But he shook his ears
and went on snorting, knee-deep in pawpaws,
trundling his hunger, shrugged off the tick-birds,
rolled up his sleeves, kicked over an anthill,
crunched, munched, wonderful windfall,
empty dish. And gored that old beat-up tin tray
for more, it stuck on his horn,
looked up with weird crown on his horn
like a bear with a beehive, began to glow —
as leerie lair bear glows honeybrown —
but he glowed
             white and
                  bright and
the safety-catches started to click in the thickets
for more. Run, holy hide — take up your armour —
Run — white horn, tin clown, crown of rain-woods,
venerable shiner! Run, run, run!

And thunders glowing like a phantom
through the bush, beating the guns
this time, but will he always
when his only camouflage
is a world of white?

Save the vulnerable shiners.
Watch the phosphorus trappers.
Smash the poisonous dish.

Aberdeen Train

Rubbing a glistening circle
on the steamed-up window I framed
a pheasant in a field of mist.
The sun was a great red thing somewhere low,
struggling with the milky scene. In the furrows
a piece of glass winked into life,
hypnotized the silly dandy; we
hooted past him with his head cocked,
contemplating a bottle-end.
And this was the last of October,
a Chinese moment in the Mearns.

Canedolia

An Off-Concrete Scotch Fantasia

oa! hoy! awe! ba! mey!

who saw?
rhu saw rum. garve saw smoo. nigg saw tain. lairg saw lagg.
rigg saw eigg. largs saw haggs. tongue saw luss. mull saw yell.
stoer saw strone. drem saw muck. gask saw noss. unst saw cults.
echt saw banff. weem saw wick. trool saw twatt.

how far?
from largo to lunga from joppa to skibo from ratho to shona from
ulva to minto from tinto to tolsta from soutra to marsco from
braco to barra from alva to stobo from fogo to fada from gigha to
gogo from kelso to stroma from hirta to spango.

what is it like there?
och it's freuchie, it's faifley, it's wamphray, it's frandy, it's
sliddery.

what do you do?
we foindle and fungle, we bonkle and meigle and maxpoffle. we
scotstarvit, armit,wormit, and even whifflet. we play at crossstobs,
leuchars, gorbals, and finfan. we scavaig, and there's aye a bit of
tilquhilly. if it's wet, treshnish and mishnish.

what is the best of the country?
blinkbonny! airgold! thundergay!

and the worst?
scrishven, shiskine, scrabster, and snizort.

listen! what's that?
catacol and wauchope, never heed them.

tell us about last night
well, we had a wee ferintosh and we lay on the quiraing. it was
pure strontian!

but who was there?
petermoidart and craigenkenneth and cambusputtock and
ecclemuchty and corriehulish and balladolly and altnacanny and
clauchanvrechan and stronachlochan and auchenlachar and
tighnacrankie and tilliebruaich and killieharra and invervannach
and achnatudlem and machrishellach and inchtamurchan and
auchterfechan and kinlochculter and ardnawhallie and
invershuggle.

and what was the toast?
schiehallion! schiehallion! schiehallion!

To Joan Eardley

Pale yellow letters
humbly straggling across
the once brilliant red
of a broken shop-face
CONFECTIO
and a blur of children
at their games, passing,
gazing as they pass
at the blur of sweets
in the dingy, cosy
Rottenrow window —
an Eardley on my wall.
Such rags and streaks
that master us! —
that fix what the pick
and bulldozer have crumbled
to a dingier dust,
the living blur
fiercely guarding
energy that has vanished,
cries filling still
the unechoing close!
I wandered by the rubble
and the houses left standing
kept a chill, dying life
in their islands of stone.
No window opened
as the coal cart rolled
and the coalman's call
fell coldly to the ground.
But the shrill children
jump on my wall.

The Starlings in George Square

I

Sundown on the high stonefields!
The darkening roofscape stirs —
thick — alive with starlings
gathered singing in the square —
like a shower of arrows they cross
the flash of a western window,
they bead the wires with jet,
they nestle preening by the lamps
and shine, sidling by the lamps
and sing, shining, they stir
the homeward hurrying crowds.
A man looks up and points
smiling to his son beside him
wide-eyed at the clamour on those cliffs —
it sinks, shrills out in waves,
levels to a happy murmur,
scatters in swooping arcs,
a stab of confused sweetness
that pierces the boy like a story,
a story more than a song.
He will never forget that evening,
the silhouette of the roofs,
the starlings by the lamps.

II

The City Chambers are hopping mad.
Councillors with rubber plugs in their ears!
Secretaries closing windows!
Window-cleaners want protection and danger money.
The Lord Provost can't hear herself think, man.
What's that?
Lord Provost, can't hear herself think.

At the General Post Office
the clerks write Three Pounds Starling in the savings-books.
Each telephone-booth is like an aviary.
I tried to send a parcel to County Kerry but —
The cables to Cairo got fankled, sir.
What's that?
I said the cables to Cairo got fankled.

And as for the City Information Bureau —
I'm sorry I can't quite chirrup did you twit —
No I wanted to twee but perhaps you can't cheep —
Would you try once again, that's better, I — sweet —
When's the last boat to Milngavie? Tweet?
What's that?
I said when's the last boat to Milngavie?

III

There is nothing for it now but scaffolding:
clamp it together, send for the bird-men,
Scarecrow Strip for the window-ledge landings,
Cameron's Repellent on the overhead wires.
Armour our pediments against eavesdroppers.
This is a human outpost. Save our statues.
Send back the jungle. And think of the joke:
as it says in the papers, It is very comical
to watch them alight on the plastic rollers
and take a tumble. So it doesn't kill them?
All right, so who's complaining? This isn't Peking
where they shoot the sparrows for hygiene and cash.
So we're all humanitarians, locked in our cliff-dwellings
encased in our repellent, guano-free and guilt-free.
The Lord Provost sings in her marble hacienda.
The Postmaster-General licks an audible stamp.
Sir Walter is vexed that his column's deserted.
I wonder if we really deserve starlings?
There is something to be said for these joyous messengers
that we repel in our indignant orderliness.
They lift up the eyes, they lighten the heart,

and some day we'll decipher that sweet frenzied whistling
as they wheel and settle along our hard roofs
and take those grey buttresses for home.
One thing we know they say, after their fashion.
They like the warm cliffs of man.

King Billy

Grey over Riddrie the clouds piled up,
dragged their rain through the cemetery trees.
The gates shone cold. Wind rose
flaring the hissing leaves, the branches
swung, heavy, across the lamps.
Gravestones huddled in drizzling shadow,
flickering streetlight scanned the requiescats,
a name and an urn, a date, a dove
picked out, lost, half regained.
What is this dripping wreath, blown from its grave
red, white, blue, and gold
'To Our Leader of Thirty years Ago' —

Bareheaded, in dark suits, with flutes
and drums, they brought him here, in procession
seriously, King Billy of Brigton, dead,
from Bridgeton Cross: a memory of violence,
brooding days of empty bellies,
billiard smoke and a sour pint,
boots or fists, famous sherrickings,
the word, the scuffle, the flash, the shout,
bloody crumpling in the close,
bricks for papish windows, get
the Conks next time, the Conks ambush
the Billy Boys, the Billy Boys the Conks till
Sillitoe scuffs the razors down the stank —
No, but it isn't the violence they remember

but the legend of a violent man
born poor, gang-leader in the bad times
of idleness and boredom, lost in better days,
a bouncer in a betting club,
a quiet man at last, dying
alone in Bridgeton in a box bed.
So a thousand people stopped the traffic
for the hearse of a folk hero and the flutes
threw 'Onward Christian Soldiers' to the winds
from unironic lips, the mourners kept
in step, and there were some who wept.

Go from the grave. The shrill flutes
are silent, the march dispersed.
Deplore what is to be deplored,
and then find out the rest.

Glasgow Green

Clammy midnight, moonless mist.
A cigarette glows and fades on a cough.
Meth-men mutter on benches,
pawed by river fog. Monteith Row
sweats coldly, crumbles, dies
slowly. All shadows are alive.
Somewhere a shout's forced out — "No!" —
it leads to nothing but silence,
except the whisper of the grass
and the other whispers that fill the shadows.

"What d'ye mean see me again?
D'ye think I came here jist for that?
I'm no finished with you yet.
I can get the boys t'ye, they're no that faur away.
You wouldny like that eh? Look there's no two ways aboot it.

Christ but I'm gaun to have you Mac
if it takes all night, turn over you bastard
turn over, I'll ——"
                        Cut the scene.
Here there's no crying for help,
it must be acted out, again, again.

This is not the delicate nightmare
you carry to the point of fear
and wake from, it is life, the sweat
is real, the wrestling under a bush
is real, the dirty starless river
is the real Clyde, with a dishrag dawn
in rinses the horrors of the night
but cannot make them clean,
though washing blows
                        where the women watch
by day,
        and children run,
                        on Glasgow Green.

And how shall these men live?
Providence, watch them go!
Watch them love, and watch them die!
How shall the race be served?
It shall be served by anguish
as well as by children at play.
It shall be served by loneliness
as well as by family love.
It shall be served by hunter and hunted in their endless chain
as well as by those who turn back the sheets in peace.
The thorn in the flesh!
Providence, water it!
Do you think it is not watered?
Do you think it is not planted?
Do you think there is not a seed of the thorn
as there is also a harvest of the thorn?
Man, take in that harvest!

Help that tree to bear its fruit!
Water the wilderness, walk there, reclaim it!
Reclaim, regain, renew! Fill the barns and the vats!

Longing,
            longing
                        shall find its wine.

Let the women sit in the Green
and rock their prams as the sheets
blow and whip in the sunlight.
But the beds of married love
are islands in a sea of desire.
Its waves break here, in this park,
splashing the flesh as it trembles
like driftwood through the dark.

In the Snack-bar

A cup capsizes along the formica,
slithering with a dull clatter.
A few heads turn in the crowded evening snack-bar.
An old man is trying to get to his feet
from the low round stool fixed to the floor.
Slowly he levers himself up, his hands have no power.
He is up as far as he can get. The dismal hump
looming over him forces his head down.
He stands in his stained beltless gaberdine
like a monstrous animal caught in a tent
in some story. He sways slightly,
the face not seen, bent down
in shadow under his cap.
Even on his feet he is staring at the floor
or would be, if he could see.
I notice now his stick, once painted white

but scuffed and muddy, hanging from his right arm.
Long blind, hunchback born, half paralysed
he stands
fumbling with the stick
and speaks:
"I want — to go to the — toilet."

It is down two flights of stairs, but we go.
I take his arm. "Give me — your arm — it's better," he says.
Inch by inch we drift towards the stairs.
A few yards of floor are like a landscape
to be negotiated, in the slow setting out
time has almost stopped. I concentrate
my life to his: crunch of spilt sugar,
slidy puddle from the night's umbrellas,
table edges, people's feet,
hiss of the coffee-machine, voices and laughter,
smell of a cigar, hamburgers, wet coats steaming,
and the slow dangerous inches to the stairs.
I put his right hand on the rail
and take his stick. He clings to me. The stick
is in his left hand, probing the treads.
I guide his arm and tell him the steps.
And slowly we go down. And slowly we go down.
White tiles and mirrors at last. He shambles
uncouth into the clinical gleam.
I set him in position, stand behind him
and wait with his stick.
His brooding reflection darkens the mirror
but the trickle of his water is thin and slow,
an old man's apology for living.
Painful ages to close his trousers and coat —
I do up the last buttons for him.
He asks doubtfully, "Can I — wash my hands?"
I fill the basin, clasp his soft fingers round the soap.
He washes, feebly, patiently. There is no towel.
I press the pedal of the drier, draw his hands
gently into the roar of the hot air.

33

But he cannot rub them together,
drags out a handkerchief to finish.
He is glad to leave the contraption, and face the stairs.
He climbs, and steadily enough.
He climbs, we climb. He climbs
with many pauses but with that one
persisting patience of the undefeated
which is the nature of man when all is said.
And slowly we go up. And slowly we go up.
The faltering, unfaltering steps
take him at last to the door
across that endless, yet not endless waste of floor.
I watch him helped on a bus. It shudders off in the rain.

The conductor bends to hear where he wants to go.
Wherever he could go it would be dark
and yet he must trust men.
Without embarrassment or shame
he must announce his most pitiful needs
in a public place. No one sees his face.
Does he know how frightening he is in his strangeness
under his mountainous coat, his hands like wet leaves
stuck to the half-white stick?
His life depends on many who would evade him.
But he cannot reckon up the chances,
having one thing to do,
to haul his blind hump through these rains of August.
Dear Christ, to be born for this!

Trio

Coming up Buchanan Street, quickly, on a sharp winter evening
a young man and two girls, under the Christmas lights —
The young man carries a new guitar in his arms,
the girl on the inside carries a very young baby,
and the girl on the outside carries a chihuahua.

And the three of them are laughing, their breath rises
in a cloud of happiness, and as they pass
the boy says, "Wait till he sees this but!"
The chihuahua has a tiny Royal Stewart tartan coat like a teapot-
holder,
the baby in its white shawl is all bright eyes and mouth like
favours in a fresh sweet cake,
the guitar swells out under its milky plastic cover, tied at the neck
with silver tinsel tape and a brisk sprig of mistletoe.
Orphean sprig! Melting baby! Warm chihuahua!
The vale of tears is powerless before you.
Whether Christ is born, or is not born, you
put paid to fate, it abdicates
                            under the Christmas lights.
Monsters of the year
go blank, are scattered back,
can't bear this march of three.

— And the three have passed, vanished in the crowd
(yet not vanished, for in their arms they wind
the life of men and beasts, and music,
laughter ringing them round like a guard)
at the end of this winter's day.

The Second Life

But does every man feel like this at forty —
I mean it's like Thomas Wolfe's New York, his
heady light, the stunning plunging canyons, beauty —
pale stars winking hazy downtown quitting-time,
and the winter moon flooding the skyscrapers, northern —
an aspiring place, glory of the bridges, foghorns
are enormous messages, a looming mastery
that lays its hands on the young man's bowels
until he feels in that air, that rising spirit

all things are possible, he rises with it
until he feels that he can never die —
Can it be like this, and is this what it means
in Glasgow now, writing as the aircraft roar
over building sites, in this warm west light
by the daffodil banks that were never so crowded and lavish —
green May, and the slow great blocks rising
under yellow tower cranes, concrete and glass and steel
out of a dour rubble it was and barefoot children gone —
Is it only the slow stirring, a city's renewed life
that stirs me, could it stir me so deeply
as May, but could May have stirred
what I feel of desire and strength
like an arm saluting a sun?

All January, all February the skaters
enjoyed Bingham's pond, the crisp cold evenings,
they swung and flashed among car headlights,
the drivers parked round the unlit pond
to watch them, and give them light, what laughter
and pleasure rose in the rare lulls
of the yards-away stream of wheels along Great Western Road!
The ice broke up, but the boats came out.
The painted boats are ready for pleasure.
The long light needs no headlamps.

Black oar cuts a glitter: it is heaven on earth.

Is it true that we come alive
not once, but many times?
We are drawn back to the image
of the seed in darkness, or the greying skin
of the snake that hides a shining one —
it will push that used-up matter off
and even the film of the eye is sloughed —
That the world may be the same, and we are not
and so the world is not the same,
the second eye is making again

this place, these waters and these towers,
they are rising again
as the eye stands up to the sun,
as the eye salutes the sun.

Many things are unspoken
in the life of a man, and with a place
there is an unspoken love also
in undercurrents, drifting, waiting its time.
A great place and its people are not renewed lightly.
The caked layers of grime
grow warm, like homely coats.
But yet they will be dislodged
and men will still be warm.
The old coats are discarded.
The old ice is loosed.
The old seeds are awake.

Slip out of darkness, it is time.

From a City Balcony

How often when I think of you the day grows bright!
Our silent love
wanders in Glen Fruin with butterflies and cuckoos —
bring me the drowsy country thing! Let it drift above the traffic
by the open window with a cloud of witnesses —
a sparkling burn, white lambs, the blaze of gorse,
the cuckoos calling madly, the real white clouds over us,
white butterflies about your hand in the short hot grass,
and then the witness was my hand closing on yours,
my mouth brushing against your eyelids and your lips
again and again till you sighed and turned for love.

Your breast and thighs were blazing like the gorse.
I covered your great fire in silence there.
We let the day grow old along the grass.
It was in the silence the love was.

Footsteps and witnesses! In this Glasgow balcony who pours
such joy like mountain water? It brims, it spills over and over
down to the parched earth and the relentless wheels.
How often will I think of you, until
our dying steps forget this light, forget
that we ever knew the happy glen,
or that I ever said, We must jump into the sun,
and we jumped into the sun.

Strawberries

There were never strawberries
like the ones we had
that sultry afternoon
sitting on the step
of the open french window
facing each other
your knees held in mine
the blue plates in our laps
the strawberries glistening
in the hot sunlight
we dipped them in sugar
looking at each other
not hurrying the feast
for one to come
the empty plates
laid on the stone together
with the two forks crossed
and I bent towards you
sweet in that air

in my arms
abandoned like a child
from your eager mouth
the taste of strawberries
in my memory
lean back again
let me love you

let the sun beat
on our forgetfulness
one hour of all
the heat intense
and summer lightning
on the Kilpatrick hills

let the storm wash the plates

One Cigarette

No smoke without you, my fire.
After you left,
your cigarette glowed on in my ashtray
and sent up a long thread of such quiet grey
I smiled to wonder who would believe its signal
of so much love. One cigarette
in the non-smoker's tray.
As the last spire
trembles up, a sudden draught
blows it winding into my face.
Is it smell, is it taste?
You are here again, and I am drunk on your tobacco lips.
Out with the light.
Let the smoke lie back in the dark.
Till I hear the very ash
sigh down among the flowers of brass
I'll breathe, and long past midnight, your last kiss.

Absence

My shadow —
I woke to a wind swirling the curtains light and dark
and the birds twittering on the roofs, I lay cold
in the early light in my room high over London.
What fear was it that made the wind sound like a fire
so that I got up and looked out half-asleep
at the calm rows of street-lights fading far below?
Without fire
only the wind blew.
But in the dream I woke from, you
came running through the traffic, tugging me, clinging
to my elbow, your eyes spoke
what I could not grasp —
Nothing, if you were here!

The wind of the early quiet
merges slowly now with a thousand rolling wheels.
The lights are out, the air is loud.
It is an ordinary January day.
My shadow, do you hear the streets?
Are you at my heels? Are you here?
And I throw back the sheets.

In Sobieski's Shield

well the prophets were dancing in the end much
good it did them and the sun didn't rise at all
anywhere but we weren't among the frozen we had been
dematerialized the day before solar withdrawal
in a hurry it's true but by the best technique
who said only technique well anyhow the best
available and here we are now rematerialized
to the best of my knowledge on a minor planet

of a sun in Sobieski's Shield in our right mind I hope
approximately though not unshaken and admittedly
not precisely those who set out if one can
speak of it by that wellworn tellurian euphemism
in any case molecular reconstitution is no
sinecure even with mice and I wouldn't have been
utterly surprised if some of us had turned out
mice or worse

but at least not that or not yet the effects
of violent change are still slightly present an
indescribable stringent sensation like perhaps being
born or dying but no neither of these I am
very nearly who I was I see I have only
four fingers on my left hand and there's a sharp
twinge I never had in my knee and one most curious
I almost said birthmark and so it is in a sense
light brown shaped like a crazy heart spreading
across my right forearm well let it be we are
here my wife my son the rest of the laboratory
my wife has those streaks of fiery red in her
hair that is expected in women she looks very
frightened yet and lies rigid the rematerialization
is slow in her but that is probably better yes
her eyes flutter to mine questioning I nod can I
smile I think I can does she see me yes thank god
she is hardly altered apart from that extraordinarily
strange and beautiful crown of bright red hair
I draw her head into my arms and hide the sobbing
shuddering first breaths of her second life I don't
know what made me use that phrase who are we
if we are not who we were we have only
one life though we are huddled now in our
protective dome on this harsh metallic plain
that belches cobalt from its craters under a
white-bronze pulsing gong of a sun it was all
they could do for us light-years away it seemed suitable
dematerialization's impossible over short distances anyway

41

so let's start moving I can surely get onto my feet
yes hoy there

my son is staring fascinated at my four fingers
you've only one nipple I tell him and it's true
but for compensation when he speaks his boy's
treble has broken and at thirteen he is a man
what a limbo to lose childhood in where has
it gone between the throwing of a switch and these
alien iron hills across so many stars his blue eyes
are the same but there's a new graveness of the
second life that phrase again we go up together
to the concave of the dome the environment after all
has to be studied

is that a lake of mercury I can't quite see
through the smoke of the fumarole it's lifting now
but there's something puzzling even when I
my memory of mercury seems to be confused with
what is it blood no no mercury's not like blood
what then what is it I'm remembering or nearly
remembering look dad mercury he says and so it
must be but I see a shell-hole filled with rain-water
red in the sinking sun I know that landscape too
one of the wars far back twentieth century I think the
great war was it called France Flanders fields I remember
reading these craters waterlogged with rain mud blood
I can see a stark hand brandishing nothing through placid scum
in a lull of the guns what horror that the livid water
is not shaken by the pity of the tattoo on the dead arm
a heart still held above the despair of the mud
my god the heart on my arm my second birth mark
the rematerialization has picked up these fragments I have
a graft of war and ancient agony forgive
me my dead helper

the sulky pool of mercury stares back at me I am
seeing normally now but I know these flashes will return

from the far past times I gather my wife and son to me
with a fierce gesture that surprises them I am not
a demonstrative man yet how to tell them
what and who I am that we are bound to all that lived
though the barriers are unspeakable we know a little of that
but something what is it gets through it is not
an essence but an energy how it pierces how it
clutches for still as I run my hand through her
amazing hair streaming on my shoulder I feel
a fist shaken in a shell-hole turn in my very marrow
we shall live in the rings of this chain the jeremiahs
who said nothing human would stand are confounded if I cry
even the dry tear in my heart that I cannot
stop or if I laugh to think they thought they
could divide the indivisible the old moon's in
the new moon's arms let's take our second
like our first life out from the dome are the suits
ready the mineral storm is quieter it's hard
to go let's go

From the Domain of Arnheim

And so that all these ages, these years
we cast behind us, like the smoke-clouds
dragged back into vacancy when the rocket springs —

The domain of Arnheim was all snow, but we were there.
We saw a yellow light thrown on the icefield
from the huts by the pines, and laughter came up
floating from a white corrie
miles away, clearly.
We moved on down, arm in arm.
I know you would have thought it was a dream
but we were there. And those were trumpets —

tremendous round the rocks —
while they were burning fires of trash and mammoths' bones.
They sang naked, and kissed in the smoke.
A child, or one of their animals, was crying.
Young men blew the ice crystals off their drums.
We came down among them, but of course
they could see nothing, on their time-scale.
Yet they sensed us, stopped, looked up — even into our eyes.
To them we were a displacement of the air,
a sudden chill, yet we had no power
over their fear. If one of them had been dying
he would have died. The crying
came from one just born: that was the cause
of the song. We saw it now. What had we stopped
but joy?
I know you felt
the same dismay, you gripped my arm, they were waiting
for what they knew of us to pass.
A sweating trumpeter took
a brand from the fire with a shout and threw it
where our bodies would have been —
we felt nothing but his courage.
And so they would deal with every imagined power
seen or unseen.
There are no gods in the domain of Arnheim.

We signalled to the ship; got back;
our lives and days returned to us, but
haunted by deeper souvenirs than any rocks or seeds.
From time the souvenirs are deeds.

What is 'Paradise Lost' Really About?

The bard has fired his bullet at the fox.
The dilatory fox is full of duck.
The gun takes brush and breakfast, quack and cluck.
Foxes in satchels are sequestered flocks.

The critic shakes the satchel with a cry.
"Your fur is feathers! You have bagged a bird!"
The simple bard is bolshy when he's stirred.
"I felled a fox, and foxes cannot fly."

Deep in the duck the maggot faintly mauls.
Viruses mill within the maggot's vein.
The photomicrograph shows fields of grain.
Down in these fields the fox's double falls.

Critics can pant across this paradox.
Critics can call the bard a blunderbuss.
Bards who have shot their shout are boisterous.
Bards have the fox's body in a box.

A View of Things

what I love about dormice is their size
what I hate about rain is its sneer
what I love about the Bratach Gorm is its unflappability
what I hate about scent is its smell
what I love about newspapers is their etaoin shrdl
what I hate about philosophy is its pursed lip
what I love about Rory is his old grouse
what I hate about Pam is her pinkie
what I love about semi-precious stones is their preciousness
what I hate about diamonds is their mink

what I love about poetry is its ion engine
what I hate about hogs is their setae
what I love about love is its porridge-spoon
what I hate about hate is its eyes
what I love about hate is its salts
what I hate about love is its dog
what I love about Hank is his string vest
what I hate about the twins is their three gloves
what I love about Mabel is her teeter
what I hate about gooseberries is their look, feel, smell, and taste
what I love about the world is its shape
what I hate about a gun is its lock, stock, and barrel
what I love about bacon-and-eggs is its predictability
what I hate about derelict buildings is their reluctance to
     disintegrate
what I love about a cloud is its unpredictability
what I hate about you, chum, is your china
what I love about many waters is their inability to quench love

Phoning

The roofs and cranes
and the dark rain

I look back
remembering an evening
we sat on the bed
and I dialled Montreux
a sudden impulse
we had to laugh
at that chain of numbers
0104121615115
Grand Hôtel des Alpes
and we spoke to your sister
Glasgow to the snows

and the sunny funiculars
and meetings by a lake
so far from Law and
the pits and cones
of worked Lanarkshire
my arm on your shoulder
held you as you spoke
your voice vibrating
as you leaned against me
remembering this
and your finger tapping
my bare knee
to emphasize a point
but most of all
in that dusky room
the back of your head
as you bent to catch
the distant words
caught my heart
vulnerable
as the love
with which I make
this sunset chain
remembering

deep in the city
far from the snows

Glasgow 5 March 1971

With a ragged diamond
of shattered plate-glass
a young man and his girl
are falling backwards into a shop-window.
The young man's face

is bristling with fragments of glass
and the girl's leg has caught
on the broken window
and spurts arterial blood
over her wet-look white coat.
Their arms are starfished out
braced for impact,
their faces show surprise, shock,
and the beginning of pain.
The two youths who have pushed them
are about to complete the operation
reaching into the window
to loot what they can smartly.
Their faces show no expression.
It is a sharp clear night
in Sauchiehall Street.
In the background two drivers
keep their eyes on the road.

Venice April 1971

Three black gondolas
cut the sparkle of the lagoon.

In the first, the Greek archimandrite
stands, a young black-bearded man
in gold cope, black hood, black shoulder veil blown back
in the sunny breeze. In front of him
his even younger acolyte holds high
the glittering processional cross. His long black robe
glitters with delicious silver flowers
against the blue of the sky.

In the second gondola Stravinsky goes.
The black fringe trails the lapping water,
the heavy coffin dips the golden lions on the sides,
the gondoliers are ankle-deep in roses,
the coffin sways crowned with roses,
the gondoliers' white blouses and black sashes
startle their brown arms, the shining oars,
the pink and crimson flowers.

And the third gondola
is like a shadow
where the widow goes.

And there at the edge of the picture
where the crowds cross themselves
and weep a little in the Italian way,
an old poet with white hair
and hooded, piercing eyes
leans on his stick
and without expression
watches the boats move out
from his shore.

London June 1970

It is opening night at Paolozzi's
crashed car exhibition.
Crowds drift and mill, drinking hard
around the hot gallery, maul
a dismal concertina'd Mini,
paw and punch a tottering A40, but
thick as flies on carrion they've clustered
about the stove-in grin
of a king-sized flare-finned 'fifties Pontiac
that squats on its own wreckage like its name.

One guest has thrown his glass at it,
smiles muzzily at the effect. Another
has crawled on the roof with a bottle,
crisscrosses claret down the shivered windscreen
with weaving hands. A third
intensely between hiccups, wrenches
a door off, you can see the sweat
spreading through his mohair.
And in the front left corner
a noted art critic nailed down
by a topless girl is slowly being
interviewed.
The interview is being viewed
in the back right corner slowly
on live closed-circuit TV.
The art of dying
is in the cars.

Glasgow November 1971

The 'speckled pipe' of the MacCrimmons,
three centuries old, is being played
in a backcourt very far from Dunvegan.
A young director of the College of Piping
is trying it out for a radio programme.
Only his cheeks show the pibroch
that rises winding into the wintry city air.
It is the long drones that are speckled,
carved in clusters of elegant bands
of creamy horn and dark brown wood,
but speckled are the high tenement walls behind them,
dark stone, pale mortar, narrow verticals
of dark window and water-pipe and pale smudge of curtains,
and speckled is the piper's kilt
against a speckled homely jungle

of grasses, thistles, dandelions, fireweed, firewood,
Capstan packets and Lanliq empties.
In a camouflage the pibroch
and the pibroch-player
disappear, half appear
MacCrimmons in Hornel.

Glasgow October 1972

At the Old Ship Bank pub in Saltmarket
a milk-lapping contest is in progress.
A dozen very assorted Bridgeton cats
have sprung from their starting-blocks
to get their heads down in the gleaming saucers.
In the middle of the picture
young Tiny is about to win his bottle of whisky
by kittening through the sweet half-gill
in one minute forty seconds flat, but
Sarah, at the end of the line,
self-contained and silver-grey,
has sat down with her back to the saucer
and surveys the photographers calmly.
She is a cat who does not like milk.

Darmstadt September 1972

A middle-aged precision instrument mechanic
having fallen behind with the mortgage repayments
on a fine new house, has kitted up
the workbench in his study
with a home-made, but well-made
guillotine, the blade

a nicely slicing two-feet-long steel
paper-trimmer, the weight
a tested squat steel
anvil, the complex of ropes
designed to release the trimmer
with a perfectly shimmering swish of
descent on his neck as he lies
prone on the bench, and
like a precision instrument
he has pulled the rope
so delicately that his head,
though severed, sits still
on the board. It looks straight
at his wife standing in the door.

Dona Ema Brazil April 1972

In a cabin of sweet cedarwood
deep in an orange-grove
an old Hungarian doctor-poet, dying,
is writing his last quirky postcard
to an English friend. His brown eyes twinkle
as he thinks of his thirteen languages,
his theory of pain, his use of hypnosis
in childbirth, his work with the Resistance
in Italy, his wryest fame in *Winnie
Ille Pu*, his end
in a nest of lianas.
With a laugh he stops
just short of the date
which who cares who will add.
ALEXANDER LENARD, says the card,
obiit, meghalt, starb, mori, died.

Andes Mountains December 1972

FUERZA AEREA URUG —
nothing more can be read on the fuselage,
tailless, wingless, a jagged cylinder
at rest in a wilderness of snow and rock.
A rugby charter from Montevideo,
the Old Christians and their supporters.
Two months after the crash, it would not seem
a bleak scene
as the sixteen tough surviving young Old Christians
crouch in the mouth of the cylinder,
sipping cups of melted snow and cherry wine,
eating quickly from plastic air force plates,
but for the yellow hands
and feet all round them
in the snow, and skulls. The plane's
fire-axe stands in today's body. The shell
where the sweet brain had been is scooped clean.
Razors have flayed the limbs in strips.
A dozen of the dead
have played their part, a dozen more
are laid out, snow-packed, in neat rows
like fish in a box. Cherry wine and blood
are as one on their chins as the flesh
they bless becomes Old Christians.

London January 1973

It is not a pile of diamonds,
it is not tons of money
that lie like a deadweight over gemsman Julius Beer.
His hideous mausoleum in Highgate Cemetery,
revealed in this journalist's flash,
is a pit of filth half filled

with pigeon-droppings and dead pigeons and
pigeons dying hundredweight on hundredweight
trapped in that poisonous cote.
Down through the broken wire of the cupola
they come, but cannot fly back out.
One flutters weakly at the top of the picture,
will soon fall into gehenna.
In the diamondman's invisible bones
nothing takes root but death.

Columba's Song

Where's Brude? Where's Brude?
So many souls to be saved!
The bracken is thick, the wildcat is quick,
the foxes dance in the moonlight,
the salmon dance in the waters,
the adders dance in the thick brown bracken.
Where's Brude? Where's man?
There's too much nature here,
eagles and deer,
but where's the mind and where's the soul?
Show me your kings, your women, the man of the plough.
And cry me to your cradles.
It wasn't for a fox or an eagle I set sail!

Floating Off to Timor

If only we'd been strangers
we'd be floating off to Timor,
we'd be shimmering on the Trades
in a blue jersey boat

with shandies, flying-fish,
a pace of dolphins
to the copra ports.
And it's no use crying
to me, What dolphins?
I know where they are
and I'd have snapped you up
and carried you away
snapped you up
and carried you away
if we had been strangers.

But here we are care
of the black roofs.
It's not hard to find
with a collar turned up
and a hoot from the Clyde.
The steps come home
whistling too. And a kettle
steams the cranes out slowly.
It's living with ships
makes a rough springtime
and who is safe
when they sing and blow
their music — they seem
to swing at some light rope
like those desires
we keep for strangers.
God, the yellow deck
breathes, it heaves spray
back like a shout.
We're cutting through
some straits of the world
in our old dark room
with salty wings
in the shriek of the dock wind.
But we're caught — meshed
in the fish-scales, ferries,

mudflats, lifebelts
fading into football cries
and the lamps coming on
to bring us in.

We take in
the dream, a cloth from the line
the trains fling sparks on
in our city. We're better awake.
But you know I'd take
you all the same,
if you were my next stranger.

In Glasgow

In my smoochy corner
take me on a cloud
I'll wrap you round
and lay you down
in smoky tinfoil
rings and records
sheets of whisky
and the moon all right
old pal all right
the moon all night

Mercy for the rainy
tyres and the violet
thunder that bring you
shambling and shy
from chains of Easterhouse
plains of lights
make your delight
in my nest my spell
my arms and my shell
my barn my bell

I've combed your hair
and washed your feet
and made you turn
like a dark eel
in my white bed
till morning lights
a silent cigarette
throw on your shirt
I lie staring yet
forget forget

The Apple's Song

Tap me with your finger,
rub me with your sleeve,
hold me, sniff me, peel me
curling round and round
till I burst out white and cold
from my tight red coat
and tingle in your palm
as if I'd melt and breathe
a living pomander
waiting for the minute
of joy when you lift me
to your mouth and crush me
and in taste and fragrance
I race through your head
in my dizzy dissolve.

I sit in the bowl
in my cool corner
and watch you as you pass
smoothing your apron.
Are you thirsty yet?
My eyes are shining.

At the Television Set

Take care if you kiss me,
you know it doesn't die.
The lamplight reaches out, draws it
blandly — all of it — into fixity,
troops of blue shadows like the soundless gunfight,
yellow shadows like your cheek by the lamp
where you lie watching, half watching
between the yellow and the blue.
I half see you, half know you.
Take care if you turn now to face me.
For even in this room we are moving out through stars
and forms that never let us back, your hand
lying lightly on my thigh and my hand on your shoulder
are transfixed only there, not here.

What can you bear that would last
like a rock through cancer and white hair?

Yet it is not easy
to take stock of miseries
when the soft light flickers
along our arms in the stillness
where decisions are made.
You have to look at me,
and then it's time that falls
talking slowly to sleep.

Blue Toboggans

scarves for the apaches
wet gloves for snowballs
whoops for white clouds
and blue toboggans

stamping for a tingle
lamps for four o'clock
steamed glass for buses
and blue toboggans

tuning-forks for Wenceslas
white fogs for Prestwick
mince pies for the Eventides
and blue toboggans

TV for the lonely
a long haul for heaven
a shilling for the gas
and blue toboggans

Lord Jim's Ghost's Tiger Poem

I can see them yet round the bungalow,
queuing up swaying and groaning slightly,
each to his steaming bowl as we had taught them —
tigers with a taste for tea were all
the rage that year at the Monsoon Club.

There was an old glade of tombs we went to
every rainy season to renew
our stock of ghosts, once brought back a rice doll,
grew into a fine peasant boy, kept our accounts —
said the old ghost in the Monsoon Club.

Lying on the rattan with pipes glowing
we saw a bird of paradise in paradise
bending to its image in an image
until a rain of diamonds was rain —
pattering white on the Monsoon Club.

The fishes in the river were choked with rice
when we came down, came down with our hooks
and threw them all back, our bottles slung
at our hips and the slurred fish sutra on our lips —
rowing back dark to the Monsoon Club.

And velvet cobras took smoke apart.
And the flute climbed above its notes.
And backs took the needle for blue tigers.
And the dead whistled through a tin sheet.
And we played go at the Monsoon Club.

Go and opium and rain! Bead-curtains
spilling round naked breasts like water!
Thunder and lacquer! All gone like that mist
framed by early morning summer doors,
my drowsy morning Monsoon Club.

I hear the slow pagoda bell.
I smell the salt of the China Sea.
I trace with the glow of my cigarette
in my hammock swinging through the straits
letters of smoke — Monsoon Club.

Hyena

I am waiting for you.
I have been travelling all morning through the bush
and not eaten.
I am lying at the edge of the bush
on a dusty path that leads from the burnt-out kraal.
I am panting, it is midday, I found no water-hole.
I am very fierce without food and although my eyes
are screwed to slits against the sun
you must believe I am prepared to spring.

What do you think of me?
I have a rough coat like Africa.
I am crafty with dark spots
like the bush-tufted plains of Africa.
I sprawl as a shaggy bundle of gathered energy
like Africa sprawling in its waters.
I trot, I lope, I slaver, I am a ranger.
I hunch my shoulders. I eat the dead.

Do you like my song?
When the moon pours hard and cold on the veldt
I sing, and I am the slave of darkness.
Over the stone walls and the mud walls and the ruined places
and the owls, the moonlight falls.
I sniff a broken drum. I bristle. My pelt is silver.
I howl my song to the moon — up it goes.
Would you meet me there in the waste places?

It is said I am a good match
for a dead lion. I put my muzzle
at his golden flanks, and tear. He
is my golden supper, but my tastes are easy.
I have a crowd of fangs, and I use them.
Oh and my tongue — do you like me
when it comes lolling out over my jaw
very long, and I am laughing?
I am not laughing.
But I am not snarling either, only
panting in the sun, showing you
what I grip
carrion with.

I am waiting
for the foot to slide,
for the heart to seize,
for the leaping sinews to go slack,
for the fight to the death to be fought to the death,

for a glazing eye and the rumour of blood.
I am crouching in my dry shadows
till you are ready for me.
My place is to pick you clean
and leave your bones to the wind.

The Loch Ness Monster's Song

Sssnnnwhufffffll?
Hnwhuffl hhnnwfl hnfl hfl?
Gdroblboblhobngbl gbl gl g g g g glbgl.
Drublhaflablhaflubhafgabhaflhafl fl fl —
gm grawwwww grf grawf awfgm graw gm.
Hovoplodok-doplodovok-plovodokot-doplodokosh?
Splgraw fok fok splgrafhatchgabrlgabrl fok splfok!
Zgra kra gka fok!
Grof grawff gahf?
Gombl mbl bl —
blm plm,
blm plm,
blm plm,
blp.

Afterwards

Afterwards the sun shone on seven rice shoots and a black tree.

Aftewards the prostitutes fell on lean times / some took up
  embroidery / one became a pearl-diver and was drowned.

Afterwards my burned little cousin went through eleven grafting
  operations / never cried.

Afterwards many saffron robes began to be let out / there was a movement to purify the order.

Afterwards the ancient monuments were restored stone by stone / I thought it was folly when I saw the list of legless girls waiting for prosthetic appliances.

Afterwards there was a report of mass ghosts on the plains, all grey as dust, with grey shovels, burying and burying all through the night to the beat of a drum / but in the morning the earth was hard and unbroken.

Afterwards came six great harvests and a glut of fish, and the rivers rolled and steamed through tunnels of fresh green fruit-trees and lilypads needled by kingfishers / rainbow after rainbow plunged into the lakes of rice.

Afterwards I went out with my sister one still hot day into the forest, and we came to an old temple bombed to a shell, with weeds in its windows, and went in hand in hand through a deep rubble of stone and fragments of half-melted statues and rubbish of metal and flowers and bread, and there in a corner we saw the skeleton of a boy, with shreds of blue cotton clinging to the bones, his fingers still clutching the string of a tiny bamboo box / we bent down as a faint chirping started from the box, and saw that it was his grasshopper, alive yet and scraping the only signal it knew from behind the bars of its cage / you said something and burst out crying / I slid the latch then and set it free.

Thoughts of a Module

It is black so. There is that dust.
My ladder in light. What are my men.
One is foot down. That is pack drill.
Black what is vizor. A hiss I heard.
The talks go up. Clump now but float.

Is a jump near. A camera paced out.
I phase another man. Another man is second.
Second last feet on. The dust I think.
So some soles cross. Is a flag near.
No move yon flag. Which voice comes down.
White house thanks all. Command module man not.
Is kangaroo hop around. I think moon dance.
Or white bird is. Good oxygen I heard.
Earth monitors must be. Is it too pressing.
Trained man is gay. Fail safe is gay.
The black I see. What instruments are lonely.
Sharp is a shadow. A horizon goes flat.
All rocks are samples. Dust taken I think.
Is bright my leg. In what sun yonder.
An end I think. How my men go.
The talks come down. The ladder I shake.
To leave that bright. Space dark I see.
Is my men last. Men are that first.
That moon is there. They have some dust.
Is home they know. Blue earth I think.
I lift I see. It is that command.
My men go back. I leave that there.
It is bright so.

The First Men on Mercury

— We come in peace from the third planet.
Would you take us to your leader?

— Bawr stretter! Bawr. Bawr. Stretterhawl?

— This is a little plastic model
of the solar system, with working parts.
You are here and we are there and we
are now here with you, is this clear?

— Gawl horrop. Bawr. Abawrhannahanna!

— Where we come from is blue and white
with brown, you see we call the brown
here 'land', the blue is 'sea', and the white
is 'clouds' over land and sea, we live
on the surface of the brown land,
all round is sea and clouds. We are 'men'.
Men come —

— Glawp men! Gawrbenner menko. Menhawl?

— Men come in peace from the third planet
which we call 'earth'. We are earthmen.
Take us earthmen to your leader.

— Thmen? Thmen? Bawr. Bawrhossop.
Yuleeda tan hanna. Harrabost yuleeda.

— I am the yuleeda. You see my hands,
we carry no benner, we come in peace.
The spaceways are all stretterhawn.

— Glawn peacemen all horrabhanna tantko!
Tan come at'mstrossop. Glawp yuleeda!

— Atoms are peacegawl in our harraban.
Menbat worrabost from tan hannahanna.

— You men we know bawrhossoptant. Bawr.
We know yuleeda. Go strawg backspetter quick.

— We cantantabawr, tantingko backspetter now!

— Banghapper now! Yes, third planet back.
Yuleeda will go back blue, white, brown
nowhanna! There is no more talk.

— Gawl han fasthapper?

65

— No. You must go back to your planet.
Go back in peace, take what you have gained
but quickly.

— Stretterworra gawl, gawl . . .

— Of course, but nothing is ever the same,
now is it? You'll remember Mercury.

Spacepoem 3: Off Course

the golden flood   the weightless seat
the cabin song   the pitch black
the growing beard   the floating crumb
the shining rendezvous   the orbit wisecrack
the hot spacesuit   the smuggled mouth-organ
the imaginary somersault   the visionary sunrise
the turning continents   the space debris
the golden lifeline   the space walk
the crawling deltas   the camera moon
the pitch velvet   the rough sleep
the crackling headphone   the space silence
the turning earth   the lifeline continents
the cabin sunrise   the hot flood
the shining spacesuit   the growing moon
    the crackling somersault   the smuggled orbit
    the rough moon   the visionary rendezvous
    the weightless headphone   the cabin debris
    the floating lifeline   the pitch sleep
    the crawling camera   the turning silence
    the space crumb   the crackling beard
    the orbit mouth-organ   the floating song

Itinerary

We went to Oldshoremore.
Is the Oldshoremore road still there?
You mean the old shore road?
I suppose it's more an old road than a shore road.
No more! They shored it up, but it's washed away.
So you could sing the old song —
Yes we sang the old song:
 We'll take the old Oldshoremore shore road no more.

We passed the Muckle Flugga.
Did you see the muckle flag?
All we saw was the muckle fog.
The flag says ULTIMA FLUGGA WHA'S LIKE US.
Couldn't see flag for fug, sorry.
Ultimately —
 Ultimately we made for Muck and flogged the lugger.

Was it bleak at Bowhousebog?
It was black as a hoghouse, boy.
Yes, but bleak?
Look, it was black as a bog and bleak as the Bauhaus!
The Bauhaus wasn't black —
Will you get off my back!
So there were dogs too?
 Dogs, hogs, leaks in the bogs — we never went back.

Not Playing the Game

— Although a poem is
undoubtedly a 'game'
it is not a game.
And although now it is even
part of the game to say so,
making it a " 'game' "
is spooky, and we'll
not play that.

— Who are you kidding, said
the next card. You just played.

— Anything I play
has no rules, if
you see the rules
it's only 'play' —
the 'dealer's eyeshade'.

— I like that smoker's cough the " 'dealer's eyeshade' ".
Your deal is showing, my dear.

— Back in the box you go in words.
'Back in the box', in other words.
Now we'll just let that
' " 'dealer's eyeshade' " '
wilt on whatever can support it, like
a poem on baize.

Rider

a grampus whacked the hydrophone / Loch Fyne left its green
  bed, fled / shrieking to Cowal / it all began
the nutcracker closed round Port Glasgow / it snapped with a
  burst of docks and / capstans downwind like collarstuds
cabbage whites in deadlock / were hanged from geans and
  rowans / wedlock-red
Greenock in steam / hammered albatrosses onto packingcases /
  without forgiveness / zam
by the waters of Glasgow / angels hung pilgrims, primroses,
  Dante, black blankets / over and over / the acid streams
a giant hedgehog lifting the Necropolis / solid silver / to the
  moon / sang of the deluge
long keys of gas unlocked the shaking Campsies at / last, at least /
  four drumlins were heard howling / as far as Fenwick Moor
Calderpark was sucked into a belljar, came out / at Kalgoorlie
  with elephants and northern lights
ravening taxis roasted dogs in basements, basted / chicken wheels
  in demolition oil / slept by the swing / of the wrecker's ball
the Holy Loch turned to granite chips, the ships / died with their
  stiff upper lips reaching to Aviemore
Para Handy sculled through the subway with the Stone of Destiny
  / shot the rapids at Cessnock right into Sunday morning
a coelacanth on stilts was setting fire to Sauchiehall Street when
  Tom Leonard /
sold James B.V. Thomson a horse, black /
in the night and dust / which galloped him away /
deep as the grave / writing

Davidson looked through the telescope at MacDiarmid and said /
  what, is that God
Davidson rode off on a blood-splashed stag / into the sea / horses
  ultimately

69

Davidson sold / fish to Neptune, fire / to Prometheus, to himself /
   a prisoner's iron bed, the red
sun rose flapping slowly over Nietzsche / bars melted into sand /
   black marias stalled in Calton
the rainbow dropped its pot of lead on Peterhead / the peter keys
   were blown to breadcrumbs, fed
to men forbid / the men bought lead, built jails, went mad, lay
   dead / in iron fields
the jaws of Nero smouldered in a dustbin / cinders tingled / the
   dead rose / tamam
sulphur shoes dancing to Mars / their zircon eyeshades flashed,
   beryllium / toeguards clipped Mercury's boulders
Lucretius was found lying under the flary walls / of a universe in
   the Crab nebula / crying
the dancers brought him water / where he lay he rose, froze / in a
   mandala like a flame / blessing
the darkness of all disbelievers / filaments of the Crab wrapped
   him in hydrogen shroud / remade
he walked by Barrhead and Vauxhall Bridge, by the sea waited /
   with his dark horse in the dangerous night air
for a rider / his testament
delivered to the earth, kicking /
the roots of things

iii

five hundred million hummingbirds sat in the Kelvin Hall / three
   hundred thousand girls took double basses
in a crocodile to Inverkip / six thousand children drew Rothesay
   through twelve thousand kites / two hundred
plumbers with morning cellos galvanized the bedmakers of
   Fairlie / forty babies
threw their teething-rings at a helicopter / trickety-track / till
   Orpheus looked back
and there was nothing but the lonely hills and sky unless the
   chilling wind was something / and the space
of pure white pain where his wife had held his hand from hell / he
   left the place

and came to a broken shack at midday / with carts and horses /
   strong dark ragged boys
played in the smoke / the gypsies gave him soup and bread / for
   the divine brooch / who cares
what is divine, he said / and passed into the valley of the Clyde,
   a cloud / followed
and many campfires in that landscape, dogs whining, cuckoos,
   glasshouses, thundershowers /
David Gray shook the rain from his hair and held his heart, the
   Luggie flashed
in the lightning of the last March storm / he led a sweet brown
   mare into the mist / the apple-boughs
closed over, where the flute
of Orpheus was only wished for /
in the drip of trees

iv

butcher-boys tried to ward off sharks / the waters rose quickly /
   great drowned bankers
floated from bay-windows / two housemaids struggled on
   Grosvenor Terrace with a giant conger
the Broomielaw was awash with slime and torn-out claws and
   anchor-flakes / rust and dust
sifted together where a dredger ploughed up the Gallowgate /
   pushed a dirty wave over Shettleston
spinning shopfronts crashed in silence / glassily, massively /
   porticoes tilting / settled in mud
lampreys fastened on four dead sailors drifting through Finnie-
   ston / in a Drygate attic
James Macfarlan threw his pen at the stinking wall / the whisky
   and the stinking poverty
ran down like ink / the well of rats was bottomless and Scotch /
   the conman and the conned
fought on / the ballads yellowed, the pubs filled / at Anderston
   he reached his grave in snow / selah
the ruined cities were switched off / there was no flood / his father
   led a pedlar's horse

by Carrick fields, his mother sang / the boy rode on a jogging
   back / far back / in rags /
Dixon's Blazes roared and threw more poets in its molten pools /
   forges on fire
matched the pitiless bread, the head
long hangdog, the lifted elbow /
the true bloody pathos and sublime

v

Kossuth took a coalblack horse from Debrecen / clattered up
   Candleriggs into the City Hall
three thousand cheers could never drown the groaning fortress-
   bars / a thousand years
heard the wind howl / scimitars, eagles, bugles, edicts, whips,
   crowns, in the pipes / playing / the grave plain in the sun
handcuffed keelies shouted in Albion Street / slogans in red
   fragments broke the cobblestones, Kossuth
drew a mirage on electric air / the hare sat calmly on the doorstep /
   it was Monday over all the world / om
Tom McGrath mixed bread and milk for the young hare / Monk
   and Parker spoke in a corner / the still room
was taken / Dougal Graham stood on his hands, the bell / rang
   between his feet / he rolled
on his hump through the swarming Tontine piazzas, swam / in
   dogs, parcels, puddles, tobacco-quids
ran with a bawbee ballad five feet long / felt fishwives / gutted
   a brace of Glasgow magistrates / lay
with a pig in his arms and cried the city fathers bitches / till a
   long shadow fell on pedlars
and far away the sound of hoofs / increased in moonlight / whole
   cities crouched in saddlebags
churches, dungeons, juntas dangled from reins / like grasses
   picked from the rank fields
and drops of halter sweat
burned men to the bone, but the hare
like mad / played

72

Stobhill

The Doctor

Yes, I agreed to perform the abortion.
The girl was under unusual strain.
I formed the opinion that for personal reasons
and home circumstances her health would suffer
if pregnancy was not terminated.
She was unmarried and the father was unknown.
She had important exams to sit,
her career would be jeopardized, and in any case
she went in mortal fear of her father
(who is himself, as it happens, a doctor)
and believed he would throw her out of the house.
These factors left me in no doubt.
Accordingly I delivered her seven months baby
without complications. It was limp and motionless.
I was satisfied there was no life in it.
Normal practice was followed: it was placed
in a paper disposal bag and sent
to the incinerator. Later to my surprise
I was told it was alive. It was then returned
and I massaged its chest and kept it warm.
It moved and breathed about eight hours.
Could it have lived? I hardly think so.
You call it a disturbing case? Disturbing
is a more emotive word than I would choose
but I take the point. However, the child
as far as I was concerned was dead
on delivery, and my disposal instructions
were straight and without melodrama.
There is, as sheriff and jury will agree,
an irony for students of the human condition
(and in this case who is not?)
in the fact that the baby was resuscitated
by the jogging of the bag on its way to the incinerator.
I hope that everything I have said is clear.

The Boilerman

Ay well, the porter brought this bag doon
(he'd come fae the operatin theatre like)
an he sayed it wis fur burnin.
Ah tellt him it would have tae wait,
ah had tae clean the fire oot first,
say hauf an oor, then it could go in.
So he goes away an leaves the bag,
it wis on a big pile of bags, like, all ready
fur tae go in. Anyway, ah gote the fire up,
ah starts throwin bags in the incinerator,
an ah'm luftin this wee bag an
ah hear a sorta whimperin — cryin like —
an ah can feel somethin breathin
through the paper. Whit did ah dae?
Ah pit it on a binch, near the hote pipes.
An ah goes up thae sterrs fur the porter.
Asks him, What wis in that bag?
He says, A foetus. Ah says, What's that?
A kiddy, he says. D'ye ken it's alive? ah says.
He says, Yes. Ah says, It's a bluidy shame,
is it no? He says, Ay it's a bluidy shame.
But the sleekit bugger never let dab
when he brought the bag. All he sayed wis burn it
and that's the God's truth. It's bad enough
whit the doctors dae, but he'd have been a murderer
if ah hadny heard the wean cryin —
Christ, it wis hingin ower the fire —
may-be a quick death in thae degrees,
but ah couldny sleep fur nights
thinkin aboot it, couldny sleep,
an och, ah still think what's the use,
ah didny save the kiddy's life.
It canny have been meant tae live.
An yet ye'd wonder, wid ye no?

The Mother

I've no idea who the father is.
I took a summer job in a hotel
in the Highlands, there was a party, I
got drunk, it must have happened then
but I remember nothing. When I knew
I was pregnant I was almost crazy,
it seemed the end of everything.
My father — it was just impossible,
you have no idea what he is like,
he would certainly have turned me out
and made my mother's life unbearable
if it wasn't unbearable before.
If I can describe him, he is a man
who equates permissive with diabolical.
Reading about a drug-raid once at breakfast
he threw a chair across the room
and swore till he was purple — swearing's
all right, and malt whisky, and chair-breaking,
but not sex. I have sometimes wondered
how he got over conceiving me,
or perhaps — if he ever did get over it.
— I am sorry, this is irrelevant.
I wanted to say that I — that my actions
are not very good and I don't defend them,
but I could not have the baby,
I just could not, you do see?
And now I never want to have one,
that's what it's done to me. I'm sick
of thinking, regretting, wishing, blaming.
I've gone so dead I see it all
like pulled from someone else's womb
and I can almost pity her
till I remember I'd be best
to forget the loss was mine.

The Father

Did she? Did she? I'm not really surprised
I'm really not. Vodka, rum, gin —
some night yon was. Was it me?
Was it my bairn? Christ, I don't know,
it might have been, I had her all right —
but there was three of us you know —
at least three — there was big Alec
and the wee French waiter wi the limp
(what d'ye cry him, Louie, wee Louie) —
and we went to this hut down by the loch —
it was a perfect night, perfect night —
mind you, we were all staggering a bit
but she was the worst let me tell you.
Big Alec, he's standing behind her and
kinna nibbling her neck and he leans over
and pulls her breasts out and says What have we here?
and she's giggling with her hair all over the place —
she looked that stupit we were all laughing —
no, I'm telling a lie, we werny all laughing,
I'll aye remember the French kid, Louie,
he wasny laughing, eyes like wee ferrets
as if he'd never seen yon before, and maybe
he hadn't, but he couldny take his eyes off her.
We got in the hut, into the hut
and see her, soon as we were in that door —
out like a light, flat on her back.
Well, I got going, then the other two,
but if you ask me they didny do much,
they'd had a right skinful and they were —
anyhow, I don't remember much after that,
it all goes a bit hazy. But I do remember
coming out the hut it was a lovely night,
it was July and it was a lovely night
with the big trees and the water an all.

76

The Porter

Ah know ah tellt them lies at the enquiry.
Ah sayed ah thought the wean wis dead
when ah took it tae the incinerator.
Ah didny think the wean wis dead,
but ah didny ken fur shair, did ah?
It's no fur me tae question the doctors.
Ah get a bag fae the sister, right?
She says take that an burn it. She's only
passin on the doctor's instructions,
but she seen the wean, she thought it wis dead,
so ye canny blame her. And the doctor says
ye canny blame him. Everybody wants
tae come doon on me like a tonna bricks.
Ah canny go aboot openin disposal bags —
if ah did ah'd be a nervous wreck.
Ah passed two electricians in the corridor
and ah tellt them the wean wis alive
but they thought ah wis jokin. Efter that
ah jist shut up, an left it tae the boilerman
tae fin oot fur hissel — he couldny miss it
could he? The puir wee thing wis squeelin
through the bag wis it no? Ah canny see
ah had tae tell him whit wis evident.
— Ah know ah'm goin on aboot this.
But suppose the kiddy could've been saved —
or suppose the boilerman hadny noticed it —
mah wee lassie's gote a hamster, ye ken? —
and ah fixed up a treadmill fur it
and it goes roon an roon an roon —
it's jist like that. Well ah'm no in court noo.
Don't answer nothin incriminatin, says the sheriff.
And that's good enough fur yours truly.
And neither ah did, neither ah did,
neither ah did, neither ah did.

Glasgow Sonnets

A mean wind wanders through the backcourt trash.
Hackles on puddles rise, old mattresses
puff briefly and subside. Play-fortresses
of brick and bric-a-brac spill out some ash.
Four storeys have no windows left to smash,
but in the fifth a chipped sill buttresses
mother and daughter the last mistresses
of that black block condemned to stand, not crash.
Around them the cracks deepen, the rats crawl.
The kettle whimpers on a crazy hob.
Roses of mould grow from ceiling to wall.
The man lies late since he has lost his job,
smokes on one elbow, letting his coughs fall
thinly into an air too poor to rob.

A shilpit dog fucks grimly by the close.
Late shadows lengthen slowly, slogans fade.
The YY PARTICK TOI grins from its shade
like the last strains of some lost *libera nos
a malo*. No deliverer ever rose
from these stone tombs to get the hell they made
unmade. The same weans never make the grade.
The same grey street sends back the ball it throws.
Under the darkness of a twisted pram
a cat's eyes glitter. Glittering stars press
between the silent chimney-cowls and cram
the higher spaces with their SOS.
Don't shine a torch on the ragwoman's dram.
Coats keep the evil cold out less and less.

iii

"See a tenement due for demolition?
I can get ye rooms in it, two, okay?
Seven hundred and nothin legal to pay
for it's no legal, see? That's my proposition,
ye can take it or leave it but. The position
is simple, you want a hoose, I say
for eight hundred pound it's yours." And they,
trailing five bairns, accepted his omission
of the foul crumbling stairwell, windows wired
not glazed, the damp from the canal, the cooker
without pipes, packs of rats that never tired —
any more than the vandals bored with snooker
who stripped the neighbouring houses, howled, and fired
their aerosols — of squeaking "Filthy lucre!"

iv

Down by the brickworks you get warm at least.
Surely soup-kitchens have gone out. It's not
the Thirties now. Hugh MacDiarmid forgot
in 'Glasgow 1960' that the feast
of reason and the flow of soul has ceased
to matter to the long unfinished plot
of heating frozen hands. We never got
an abstruse song that charmed the raging beast.
So you have nothing to lose but your chains,
dear Seventies. Dalmarnock, Maryhill,
Blackhill and Govan, better sticks and stanes
should break your banes, for poets' words are ill
to hurt ye. On the wrecker's ball the rains
of greeting cities drop and drink their fill.

v

"Let them eat cake" made no bones about it.
But we say let them eat the hope deferred
and that will sicken them. We have preferred
silent slipways to the riveters' wit.

And don't deny it — that's the ugly bit.
Ministers' tears might well have launched a herd
of bucking tankers if they'd been transferred
from Whitehall to the Clyde. And smiles don't fit
either. "There'll be no bevvying" said Reid
at the work-in. But all the dignity you muster
can only give you back a mouth to feed
and rent to pay if what you lose in bluster
is no more than win patience with "I need"
while distant blackboards use you as their duster.

vi

The North Sea oil-strike tilts east Scotland up,
and the great sick Clyde shivers in its bed.
But elegists can't hang themselves on fled-
from trees or poison a recycled cup —
If only a less faint, shaky sunup
glimmered through the skeletal shop and shed
and men washed round the piers like gold and spread
golder in soul than Mitsubishi or Krupp —
The images are ageless but the thing
is now. Without my images the men
ration their cigarettes, their children cling
to broken toys, their women wonder when
the doors will bang on laughter and a wing
over the firth be simply joy again.

vii

Environmentalists, ecologists
and conservationists are fine no doubt.
Pedestrianization will come out
fighting, riverside walks march off the lists,
pigeons and starlings be somnambulists
in far-off suburbs, the sandblaster's grout
multiply pink piebald facades to pout
at sticky-fingered mock-Venetianists.
Prop up's the motto. Splint the dying age.
Never displease the watchers from the grave.

80

Great when fake architecture was the rage,
but greater still to see what you can save.
The gutted double fake meets the adage:
a wig's the thing to beat both beard and shave.

Meanwhile the flyovers breed loops of light
in curves that would have ravished tragic Toshy —
clean and unpompous, nothing wishy-washy.
Vistas swim out from the bulldozer's bite
by day, and banks of earthbound stars at night
begin. In Madame Emé's Sauchie Haugh, she
could never gain in leaves or larks or sploshy
lanes what's lost in a dead boarded site —
the life that overspill is overkill to.
Less is not more, and garden cities are
the flimsiest oxymoron to distil to.
And who wants to distil? Let bus and car
and hurrying umbrellas keep their skill to
feed ukiyo-e beyond Lochnagar.

It groans and shakes, contracts and grows again.
Its giant broken shoulders shrug off rain.
It digs its pits to a shauchling refrain.
Roadworks and graveyards like their gallus men.
It fattens fires and murders in a pen
and lets them out in flaps and squalls of pain.
It sometimes tears its smoky counterpane
to hoist a bleary fist at nothing, then
at everything, you never know. The west
could still be laid with no one's tears like dust
and barricaded windows be the best
to see from till the shops, the ships, the trust
return like thunder. Give the Clyde the rest.
Man and the sea make cities as they must.

From thirtieth floor windows at Red Road
he can see choughs and samphires, dreadful trade —
the schoolboy reading *Lear* has that scene made.
A multi is a sonnet stretched to ode
and some say that's no joke. The gentle load
of souls in clouds, vertiginously stayed
above the windy courts, is probed and weighed.
Each monolith stands patient, ah'd and oh'd.
And stalled lifts generating high-rise blues
can be set loose. But stalled lives never budge.
They linger in the single-ends that use
their spirit to the bone, and when they trudge
from closemouth to laundrette their steady shoes
carry a world that weighs us like a judge.

The World

1

I don't think it's not going onward,
though no one said it was a greyhound.
I don't accept we're wearing late.

I don't see the nothing some say anything
that's not in order comes to be found.
It may be nothing to be armour-plated.

I don't believe that what's been made
clutters the spirit. Let it be patented
and roll. It never terrorized

three ikon angels sitting at a table
in Moscow, luminous as a hologram
and blessing everything from holograms

to pliers at a dripping nail.
I don't believe it's not the wrench
of iron that let the body fall.

2

There was this unholy scuffle.
They felled the sober with the tipsy.
At last someone got pushed mildly

onto a breadknife. As he observed
in the ward, What's more, what's more,
just nobody's going to go there.

They did though. Even if which was which
was always a guessing-game, the case
meant the whole scene had bristles on.

Expressionless hardmen glittered. Sleepwalkers
jived. There was a dog. Before
the end of the evening a desire

for everything had returned, very
smoky it's true. The sleeper
in the ward was the only one with nightmares.

3

Sometimes it swells like the echo of a passion
dying with paeans, not sighs. Who
knows the weight and list of its rebellions?

Underneath, underneath, underneath, underneath —
you think it beats in the age-old fashion,
even red, perhaps, like a pre-set strawberry

creeping below the crust? It's artistic
to have ordered impulses. To
think the world has makes you feel great.

83

Beyond the world, the slow-dying sun
flares out a signal fan, projecting
a million-mile arm in skinny hydrogen

to flutter it at our annals.
Coarse, knee-deep in years, we
go on counting, miss the vast unreason.

4

Technologies like dragonflies, the strange
to meet the strange; and at the heart
of things, who knows what is dependent?

Imagine anything the world could, it might
do; anything not to do, it would.
A plume of act flies as it spins by.

We saw the nettles in the ancient station.
The signalbox was like a windmill, haunted
by bats and autumn wasps. She

twirled a scarf through leaves. Remembrance
offered nothing, swam in our hands.
We're here. The past is not our home.

I don't think it's not being perfect
that brings the sorrows in, but being soon
beyond the force not to be powerless.

Shaker Shaken

[The first stanza is a Shaker sound-poem of 1847]

Ah pe-an t-as ke t-an te loo
O ne vas ke than sa-na was-ke
    lon ah ve shan too
Te wan-se ar ke ta-ne voo te
    lan se o-ne voo

Te on-e-wan tase va ne woo te wan-se o-ne van
Me-le wan se oo ar ke-le van te
    shom-ber on vas sa la too lar var sa
    re voo an don der on v-tar loo-cum an la voo
O be me-sum ton ton ton tol-a wac-er tol-a wac-er
    ton ton te s-er pane love ten poo

Ah pe-an t-as ke t-an tiger
O ne vas ke than tuft of was-ke
    lon ah ve shan tree
Te wan-se ar ke ta-ne voodoo
    lan se opal voo
Te on-e-wan likely va ne woo te wan-se o-ne stonework
Me-le white se oo ar ke-le van off
    shom-ber blown over sa la too lar var sa
    following an don der on opal loo-cum an la voo
O be me-sum ton ton mixed with a wac-er tol-a wac-er
    ton ton tiger pane love ten poo

That pe-an t-as saw t-an tiger
O ne vas through a tuft of was-ke
    by the ve shan tree
Nothing ar ke ta-ne voodoo
    till se opal voo
Nothing on-e-wan likely to ne woo to wan-se o-ne stonework
till a white se oo ar ke-le us off
    shom-ber blown over the la too without harm
    following an don der on opal losing our voo
O be me-sum ton ton mixed with the waters the tol-a wac-er
    ton ton tiger swam with us loved ten poo

That was when t-as saw the tiger
O ne vas through a tuft of morning-glory
    by the ve scraped tree
Nothing in the air ta-ne voodoo
    till the opal voo
Nothing seemed likely to ne woo te wan-se old stonework
till a white lot of ar ke-le us off

85

shom-ber blown over the lake without harm
following flakes on opal losing our tracks
O be me-sum and we mixed with the waters the wily waters
till the tiger swam with us loved ten poo

That was when we saw the tiger
yawning through a tuft of morning-glory
by the well-scraped tree
Nothing in the air suggested voodoo
till the opal fell
Nothing seemed likely to go warmer than old stonework
till a white lot of flame took us off
suddenly blown over the lake without harm
following flakes of opal losing our tracks
in tiger's-eyes and we mixed with the waters the wily waters
till the tiger swam with us and loved us up

Vico's Song

the universe that turned in on itself
turned in on itself
on itself
self was
was the universe
that was turned in
it was the universe that was turned in

the universe that was turned in
turned in got seven
seven days
days it
it spent turning
spent turning over
days it spent turning over a new leaf

the universe that turned over a new leaf
turned over a new leaf
new leaf
leaf lived
lived in the arms
in the arms of the eternal
it lived in the arms of the eternal return

Resurrections

None of your jade suits, none of your gold-sewn princes! —
green-shelled spoonfuls of dust like coelacanths in tombs.
I want to be born again. Keep Tollund peat
for roses, boots, blazes. Men of Han, princesses,
yellowing demons and mummies, casket-crowders,
haunt off! There's never armour made
I'd pray to be preserved in. Don't preserve me!
Yesterday great Chou's ashes flew
in the wind over plain and river,
never resting or rusting, nothing
for an urn. Unknown he blows
like seed, is seed,
a little cinnamon of the millennium.
Let them roll away the black diorite
where millions shuffle past a husk.
What? Christ too like Chou could not be found.
In this strange January spring,
so mild the blackbirds go mad
singing in the morning above Anniesland,
I woke, I heard them, no one at my side,
but thought of you with the exhilaration
of that rising song where like them I scatter
and swoop in rings over the half-dark earth,
caught up in another life.

Particle Poems

The old old old old particle
smiled. "I grant you I'm not beautiful,"
he said, "but I've got charm.
It's charm that's led me where I am."

Opened up his bosom, showed me a quark.
It gleamed. He grinned like a clam. "Sort
of heart, really, though I've got four.
They're in orbit, and what for

is a good question, unless to pump up
charm. I know I must look a frump
— just fishing — but seriously
would you not say I'm easily

the nearest thing to doom and centrehood
you've ever been unable to preclude?
Cathedrals — oh, antiquities and slime,
knucklebones, teeth five feet long, signs

and wonders, auks, knuckledusters,
twangs from armchairs, waters
waiting to break, cells waiting to squeak,
a sniff of freesia, a book

of hours, and hours themselves like days
in love, and even nanoseconds raised
by charm to higher powers, wait
until I make them, and fade."

Shot off — never showed his age.

2

The young particle screamed round the bend,
braked hard, broke.
His mother dozing in Manchuria
heard his last cry. A mare's ear twitched.
Dust, and dust, the wires sang.

3

Three particles lived in mystical union.
They made knife, fork, and spoon,
and earth, sea, and sky.
They made animal, vegetable, and mineral,
and faith, hope, and charity.
They made stop, caution, go,
and hickory, dickory, dock.
They made yolk, white, and shell,
and hook, line, and sinker.
They made pounds, shillings, and pence,
and Goneril, Regan, and Cordelia.
They made Shadrach, Meshach, and Abednego,
and game, set, and match.

A wandering particle kidnapped one of them,
and the two that were left made day and night,
and left and right, and right and wrong,
and black and white, and off and on,
but things were never quite the same,
and two will always yearn for three.
They're after you, or me.

4

Part particle and part idea, she
struggled through a throb of something.
A wheatear, or an ear of wheat?
How could she possibly know
beyond the shrill vibrations, sunny fibres, field?
What was the field but forces, surges?

To veins of green and veins of red
she was colour-blind. Well, she was blind.
But was she there at all —
when the wind ruffled that nest of growing things
and it took its course in the sun?

5

The particle that decided
got off its mark, but died.

6

Their mausoleum
is a frozen silent flak.
The fractured tracks,
photographed, docket
dead dogfights,
bursts of no malice.
Almost pure direction
points its stream,
deflected, detected.
Better than ogam
or cuneiform the tracer
of telling particles
fans out angrily
itself, itself, itself —
who we were
were here, here,
we died at the crossroads
or we defected
or we raced ahead
to be burnt out.
Faint paths hardly score,
yet shake the lens, end
in lucider mosaics
of theory. Go,
bid the soldiers shoot.

A Home in Space

Laid-back in orbit, they found their minds.
They found their minds were very clean and clear.
Clear crystals in swarms outside were their fireflies and larks.
Larks they were in lift-off, swallows in soaring.
Soaring metal is flight and nest together.
Together they must hatch.
Hatches let the welders out.
Out went the whitesuit riggers with frames as light as air.
Air was millions under lock and key.
Key-ins had computers wild on Saturday nights.
Nights, days, months, years they lived in space.
Space shone black in their eyes.
Eyes, hands, food-tubes, screens, lenses, keys were one.
One night — or day — or month — or year — they all —
all gathered at the panel and agreed —
agreed to cut communication with —
with the earth base — and it must be said they were —
were cool and clear as they dismantled the station and —
and gave their capsule such power that —
that they launched themselves outwards —
outwards in an impeccable trajectory, that band —
that band of tranquil defiers, not to plant any —
any home with roots but to keep a —
a voyaging generation voyaging, and as far —
as far as there would ever be a home in space —
space that needs time and time that needs life.

The Mouth

I saw a great mouth in space that fifty thousand angels could not
    fill
they ran shrieking from it as it grew and threw their coloured
    coats and flares

for lures among the stars while it advanced and swallowed the
    planets of the sun
one by one and then the sun

it rose and swayed the Milky Way collapsed into it like a poorly
    shuffled pack
deeper and deeper into darkness it brought darkness and what it
    blotted out
it grew drunk on to grinning-point with so much fire in its belly
    it roared
over its thankless hoard

for that was the new horror to hear it when it howled like a hungry
    scraped womb
and galaxies jampacked with glittering rayed-out million-year-old
    civilizations
were jumped like a handful of asteroids and sucked into tales of
    hell
for all they could tell

the Plough long gone the winding Dragon the Lyre the Balance
    the fading Charioteer
Aquarius with a loud cry Keel Stern and Sails in terrible rushing
    silence
and now white Sirius was black yellow Capella was black red
    Antares was black
and no lights ever came back

heavens and paradises popped like seaweed eternal laws were
    never seen again
angels' teeth were cosmic dust and cosmic dust was angels' teeth
    all's grist
to that dark mill where christs and godbearers were pulped with
    their domes ikons vanes
their scrolls aeons and reigns

in Virgo the most evolved life there was was calm and watchful in
    its fiery coverts

the mouth had long been computed probable and plans had been
 laid and re-laid
the dense cluster of three thousand galaxies had made itself a force
 field
that would not know how to yield

the worlds of Virgo were not only inhabited but hyperinhabited
 they were all
one life and their force field was themselves they were a wall they
 shone they stood
jehovahs and elohim are daguerreotypes to their movies they
 made universes
as poets make verses

in Virgo they did not underestimate the mouth they were the last
 star-gate and goal
when they saw there were no other lights in the recesses of space
 and it was hard
to distinguish the shadow of the unsated mouth from the shadow
 of the dead
but its lips were blackest red

they gaped for Virgo with a scream they gaped for Virgo with a
scream they gaped for Virgo with a scream they gaped for Virgo
with a scream they gaped for Virgo with a scream they gaped
at that great quiet gate

The Moons of Jupiter

Amalthea, Io, Europa, Ganymede, Callisto

Amalthea

I took a book with me to Amalthea
but never turned a page. It weighed like lead.
I squatted with it like a grey image
malleted into the rock, listlessly

reading, staring, rereading listlessly
sentences that never came to anything.
My very memory lay paralysed
with everything else on that bent moon,
pulled down and dustbound, flattened, petrified
by gravitation, sweeping Jupiter's
more than half the sky with sentences
half-formed that never came to anything.
My tongue lay like a coil of iron, the planet
never heard a word. What did I say there?
My very memory is paralysed.
The book has gone too — I know how it began
but that first sentence never came to anything.
"The local train, with its three coaches, pulled up
at Newleigh Station at half-past four . . ."
The tons of pages never moved, my knees
were tombs, and though slow Jupiter slid past,
my memory of it is paralysed.
The stupid moon goes round. The local train,
with its three coaches pulled up at Newleigh Station
at half-past four, never comes to anything.
They rescued me with magnets, plucked me up
like dislocated yards of groaning mandrake.
The satellite engulfed the book in dust.

Io

The sulphur mines on Io were on strike
when we arrived. I can't say I'm surprised.
Seventy-five men had just been killed
in the fiercest eruption ever seen there.
I hardly recognized the grim volcano
with its rakish new crater and a leaning plume
two hundred miles high — like an ash tree,
someone said. Meanwhile the landscape burned,
not that it never burned before, but this
was roaring, sheeted, cruel. Empty
though not perfunctory funeral rites
had been performed; not a body was found.

The weird planetman's flute from friends in grief —
my god what a strange art it is, rising
so many million miles from home into
the raw thin cindery air — was the first sound
we heard when we stepped from the ship. We saw
the men huddled in knots, or walking slowly
with bent heads over the pumice beds, or still
and silent by the bank of the red lake.
The laser probes, the belts, the brilliant console
sat dark and motionless, crawled through by smoke.
Sulphur blew to choke the very soul.
We prospected beyond the lava-fields,
but the best sulphur's the most perilous.
The planetman must shoulder sorrow, great sacks
of pain, in places with no solace but
his own and what the winds and days may bring.

Europa

Boots and boats — in our bright orange gear
we were such an old-fashioned earthly lot
it seemed almost out of time-phase. We learned
or re-learned how to skate and ski, use snowshoes,
fish through ice-holes though not for fish. Soundings
and samples were our prey. We'd never grade
in years, far less in weeks, the infinite
play and glitter of watery Europa,
waters of crust ice, waters of deep ice,
waters of slush, of warm subcrustal springs,
waters of vapour, waters of water.
One day, and only one, we drilled right down
to something solid and so solid-hard
the drill-head screamed into the microphone
and broke, the film showed streaks of metal shards
whizzing across a band of basalt or
glimmery antediluvian turtle-shell
or cast-off titan miner's helmet or —
it must have been the metal scream that roused
our thought and fear and half desire we might

have had a living scream returned. Lightly
it sleeps, the imagination. On that smooth moon
men would be driven mad with many dreams,
hissing along the hill-less shining wastes,
or hearing the boat's engine chug the dark
apart, as if a curtain could be drawn
to let the living see even the dead
if they had once had life, if not that life.

Ganymede

Galileo would have been proud of Ganymede.
Who can call that marbled beauty dead?
Dark basins sweeping to a furrowed landfall,
gigantic bright-rayed craters, vestiges
and veils of ice and snow, black swirling grey,
grey veined with green, greens diffused in blues,
blue powdered into white: a king marble
rolled out, and set in place, from place to place.
We never landed, only photographed
and sent down probes from orbit; turbulence
on Jupiter was extreme, there was no lingering.
Is it beauty, or minerals, or knowledge
we take our expeditions for? What a question!
But is it What a question? Is it excitement,
or power, or understanding, or illumination
we take our expeditions for? Is it specimens,
or experiments, or spin-off, or fame, or evolution,
or necessity we take our expeditions for?
We are here, and our sons or our sons' sons
will be on Jupiter, and their sons' sons
at the star gate, leaving the fold of the sun.
I remember I drowsed off, dropped my notes,
with the image of Ganymede dancing before me.
They nudged me, smiling, said it was a judgement
for my wandering thoughts, what had got into me?
That satellite had iron and uranium.
We would be back. Well, that must be fine,
I teased them; had it gold, and asphodel?

Callisto

Scarred, cauterized, pocked and warty face:
you grin and gape and gawk and cock an ear
at us with craters, all blind, all deaf, all dumb,
toadback moon, brindled, brown and cold,
we plodded dryshod on your elephant-hide seas
and trundled gear from groove to groove, playing
the record of your past, imagining
the gross vales filled with unbombarded homes
they never had till we pitched nylon tents there:
radiation falling by the ton,
but days of meteorites long gone. Scatter
the yellow awnings, amaze the dust and ochre!
Frail and tough as flags we furnish out
the desolation. Even the greatest crater,
gouged as if a continent had struck it,
circled by rim on rim of ridges rippling
hundreds of miles over that slaty chaos,
cannot forbid our feet, our search, our songs.
I did not sing; the grave-like mounds and pits
reminded me of one grave long ago
on earth, when a high Lanarkshire wind
whipped out the tears men might be loath to show,
as if the autumn had a mercy I
could not give to myself, listening in shame
to the perfunctory priest and to my thoughts
that left us parted on a quarrel. These
memories, and love, go with the planetman
in duty and in hope from moon to moon.

The Mummy

(The mummy [*of Rameses II*] was met at Orly airport by Mme Saunier-Seïté. — *News item, Sept. 1976*)

— May I welcome Your Majesty to Paris.

— Mm.

— I hope the flight from Cairo was reasonable.

— Mmmmm.

— We have a germ-proof room at the Museum of Man
   where we trust Your Majesty will have peace and quiet.

— Unh-unh.

— I am sorry, but this is necessary.
   Your Majesty's person harbours a fungus.

— Fng fng's, hn?

— Well, it is something attacking your cells.
   Your Majesty is gently deteriorating
   after nearly four thousand years
   becalmed in masterly embalmment.
   We wish to save you from the worm.

— Wrm hrm! Mgh-mgh-mgh.

— Indeed I know it must be distressing
   to a pharaoh and a son of Ra,
   to the excavator of Abu Simbel
   that glorious temple in the rock,
   to the perfecter of Karnak hall,
   to the hammer of the Hittites,
   to the colossus whose colossus

raised in red granite at holy Thebes
sixteen-men-high astounds the desert
shattered, as Your Majesty in life
shattered the kingdom and oppressed the poor
with such lavish grandeur and panache,
to Rameses, to Ozymandias,
to the Louis Quatorze of the Nile,
how bitter it must be to feel
a microbe eat your camphored bands.
But we are here to help your Majesty.
We shall encourage you to unwind.
You have many useful years ahead.

— M' n'm 'z 'zym'ndias, kng'v kngz!

— Yes yes. Well, Shelley is dead now.
He was not embalmed. He will not write
about Your Majesty again.

— T't'nkh'm'n? H'tsh'ps't?
'khn't'n? N'f'rt'ti? Mm? Mm?

— The hall of fame has many mansions.
Your Majesty may rest assured
your deeds will always be remembered.

— Youmm w'm'nn. B't'flll w'm'nnnn.
No w'm'nnn f'r th'zndz y'rz.

— Your Majesty, what are you doing?

— Ng! Mm. Mhm. Mm? Mm? Mmmmm.

— Your Majesty, Your Majesty! You'll break your stitches!

— Fng st'chez fng's wrm hrm.

— I really hate to have to use
  a hypodermic on a mummy,
  but we cannot have you strain yourself.
  Remember your fungus, Your Majesty.

— Fng. Zzzzzzzz.

— That's right.

— Aaaaaaaaah.

Instructions to an Actor

Now, boy, remember this is the great scene.
You'll stand on a pedestal behind a curtain,
the curtain will be drawn, and then you don't move
for eighty lines; don't move, don't speak, don't breathe.
I'll stun them all out there, I'll scare them,
make them weep, but it depends on you.
I warn you eighty lines is a long time,
but you don't breathe, you're dead,
you're a dead queen, a statue,
you're dead as stone, new-carved,
new-painted and the paint not dry
— we'll get some red to keep your lip shining —
and you're a mature woman, you've got dignity,
some beauty still in middle age, and
you're kind and true, but you're dead,
your husband thinks you're dead,
the audience thinks you're dead,
and you don't breathe, boy, I say
you don't even blink for eighty lines,
if you blink you're out!
Fix your eye on something and keep watching it.
Practise when you get home. It can be done.

And you move at last — music's the cue.
When you hear a mysterious solemn jangle
of instruments, make yourself ready.
Five lines more, you can lift a hand.
It may tingle a bit, but lift it —
slow, slow —
O this is where I hit them
right between the eyes, I've got them now —
I'm making the dead walk —
you move a foot, slow, steady, down,
you guard your balance in case you're stiff,
you move, you step down, down from the pedestal,
control your skirt with one hand, the other hand
you now hold out —
O this will melt their hearts if nothing does —
to your husband who wronged you long ago
and hesitates in amazement
to believe you are alive.
Finally he embraces you, and there's nothing
I can give you to say, boy,
but you must show that you have forgiven him.
Forgiveness, that's the thing. It's like a second life.
I know you can do it. — Right then, shall we try?

Migraine Attack

We had read about the reed-beds but went on
right through the night. With blades as sharp as that
you scarcely feel the cuts, and blood in darkness
is merely darkness. Oh there was moonlight
in fits and starts, but it confused us more
than it ever illuminated, as we kept moving
under the jagged filter of the forest ceiling —
whatever light there was made convicts of us,
frisked us, left us stumbling through our chains

of shadows. From our feet — shadows,
from our rifles — shadows, from branches —
shadows like bats and bats like shadows.
Sometimes the treetop mat was thick with mosses,
creepers, ancient nests, a stamping-ground
for upside-down explorers going to heaven:
we really saw them there, in our delirium,
riding on giant sloths, with their rags of clothes
and raddled hair streaming down to gravity.
They passed; the scrunts and scrogs passed; snakes passed;
eyes and beaks in bushes passed; a long wing passed;
the scuttlings and the slitherings and the roars
passed; time, even, as they passed, must have passed.
We were moving columns of sweat and crusted blood,
burrs, leaf-mould, mud, mosquitoes, map-cases
and a bandage or two as we leaned into it
to defeat it, and the wood grew grey
as it gave up and felt
the distant day, thinned out
to glades threaded by mist
sent from the unseen sun.
We shook ourselves like dogs
and tried a song.

Winter

The year goes, the woods decay, and after,
many a summer dies. The swan
on Bingham's pond, a ghost, comes and goes.
It goes, and ice appears, it holds,
bears gulls that stand around surprised,
blinking in the heavy light, bears boys
when skates take over swan-tracks gone.
After many summer dyes, the swan-white ice
glints only crystal beyond white. Even

dearest blue's not there, though poets would find it.
I find one stark scene
cut by evening cries, by warring air.
The muffled hiss of blades escapes into breath,
hangs with it a moment, fades off.
Fades off, goes, the scene, the voices fade,
the line of trees, the woods that fall, decay
and break, the dark comes down, the shouts
run off into it and disappear.
At last the lamps go too, when fog
drives monstrous down the dual carriageway
out to the west, and even in my room
and on this paper I do not know
about that grey dead pane
of ice that sees nothing and that nothing sees.

Surrealism Revisited

An avuncular mussel stamped its foot and the sea took an attack
of vertigo as far as it would go.
A dictionary without happiness was shot down as it gave a perfect
bound over the heights of hands.
A caryatid ate a parrot with traffic jam.
A penthouse laid a bad egg and the prime minister took it to the
country.
A crate of brandy snaps was driven mad by a strike of cream.
A giant wheel was arrested for blasphemy as it tried to thread a
needle.
An interurban flyover turned into an old hag in broad daylight
and was dismembered by cranes.
A bag of sleet was found in a blast furnace.
An ant's egg filled with speculators was detonated by remote
control.
A silver centaur ridden by a golden boy plunged through the sky
screaming for paint-stripper.

103

A clockwork orange by Fabergé fell out of a magpie's nest and ate
    humble pie.
A brazen yelp escaped from a condemned gasholder and was torn
    to pieces in a fight between scavengers and demons.
A book two miles high with phosphorescent letters in an unknown
    language stopped shipping in the channel for four days.
A cat barked and was deported.

On the Water

There is something almost but not quite
beguiling about the thought of houseboat days.
Creaking, lapping, a sense of sway and the illusion
of moving might be the romance of a weekend.
Toy cabins, timeless horizontal afternoons
might at last get through Proust, while she
reverses roles at a punchbag on deck,
knocks herself groggy, takes to cushions
as the sun goes down. These scenes
would only be for laughter though. Who is to make
the omelette, the one with throbbing shoulder or
the one dozy-eyed from Combray
on his back with a paper-knife,
reading against the light? The strenuous things
are great gods, bored by windows giving on water,
and even pretty hands trailed in water
knit nothing, and ask nothing to be done.
Life came from seas, lakes? It must be a joke.
The sluggish firth, like the latest bandage,
melts into the body of the earth,
cannot even sustain conversation.
It would be a breach to crow over a slammed chessman,
let alone slot in the Flying Dutchman cassette
they'd be sure to pack, these chained wanderers.
They dream, in fits and starts; it is only then

that the boat drifts, right down
to the sea and the keen wind, only then
that great gods clap their wings, and he designs
an airport, she a house and
a dress she stands in at the door to welcome
many guests and set parties ablaze.

On the Needle's Point

Of course it is not a point at all.
We live here, and we should know.
I doubt indeed if there can be a point
in created things: the finest honing
uncovers more rough. Our ground stretches
for several miles, it is like living
on an asteroid, a bounded island
but with a bottomless core lost in mist
so far below and out of sight we feel
like pillar saints in earthly Syria.
The surface is slashed and pitted, greyish
with streaks of black and enigmatic
blue silver; spores of red lichen
gather and smoulder in crevices and caves.
At the edge it is very prodigious.
We have had some climbing over and down
with home-made crampons, disappearing,
perhaps making it to what we cannot imagine;
others fly off with fixed smiles,
vanish in their elation into violet haze.
But I like it on the point, good
is the dark cavern, good the craggy walks,
good the vertiginous bare brightness,
good the music, good the dance

when sometimes we join wings and drift
in interlinking circles, how many thousands
I could never tell, silent ourselves,
almost melting into light.

The Coals

Before my mother's hysterectomy
she cried, and told me she must never bring
coals in from the cellar outside the house,
someone must do it for her. The thing itself
I knew was nothing, it was the thought
of that dependence. Her tears shocked me
like a blow. As once she had been taught,
I was taught self-reliance, discipline,
which is both good and bad. You get things done,
you feel you keep the waste and darkness back
by acts and acts and acts and acts and acts,
bridling if someone tells you this is vain,
learning at last in pain. Hardest of all
is to forgive yourself for things undone,
guilt that can poison life — away with it,
you say, and it is loath to go away.
I learned both love and joy in a hard school
and treasure them like the fierce salvage of
some wreck that has been built to look like stone
and stand, though it did not, a thousand years.

Little Blue Blue

(misprinted title of Norman MacCaig's poem
'Little Boy Blue' in *The Equal Skies*, 1980)

The mirror caught him as he straightened his sky-blue tie,
he was the son of sky and sea, five
feet high with wings furled, flexing
and shifting the sheen of his midnight blue
mohair tuxedo, tightening his saxe plastic belt
one notch, slicing the room with Gillette-blue eyes,
padding to the door in dove-blue brushed suede boots,
pinning his buttonhole periwinkle with a blue shark's grin.

    Once in the street
    he got the beat
    unfurled his wing
    began to sing
    "She is, he is, she is my star"
    to his electric blue guitar.

Little Blue Blue flew to the land of denim,
bought himself jeans and a denim jacket and a denim cap,
what blue, what blue, he cried, and tried his jeans
with his mohair dinner-jacket, tried his mohair trousers
with his denim bomber jacket, tried his denim cap
with his saxe-blue belt and his dove-blue boots and a
navy-blue Adidas bag and nothing else
till the slate-blue pigeons all blushed purple, but

    once in the street
    he got the beat
    unfurled his wing
    began to sing
    "He is, she is, he is my star"
    to his electric blue guitar.

Then he went to sea and sailed the blue main
in his navy jersey with his wings well battened down,

knocked up a tattoo parlour in old Yokohama,
got bluebirds on his hands and a blue pierced heart,
and a geisha-girl on his shoulder with a blue rose,
and a trail of blue hounds chasing a blue fox
into covert — oh, he said, I'm black and blue all over,
but he staggered out into that Nippon moon, and

> once in the street
> he got the beat
> unfurled his wing
> began to sing
> "She is, he is, she is my star"
> to his electric blue guitar.

Back home, he bought a cobalt Talbot Sunbeam
with aquamarine upholstery and citizens band radio,
said Blue Blue here, do you read me, do you read me?
as he whizzed up to Scrabster in his royal-blue pinstripes.
And his dashboard sent him messages without measure,
for everybody loves a blue angel, whistling
at the wheel under azure highland skies.
And he stopped at each village, and smiled like the sun, for

> once in the street
> he got the beat
> unfurled his wing
> began to sing
> "He is, she is, he is my star"
> to his electric blue guitar.

Grendel

> It is being nearly human
> gives me this spectacular darkness.
> The light does not know what to do with me.
> I rise like mist and I go down like water.

I saw them soused with wine behind their windows.
I watched them making love, twisting like snakes.
I heard a blind man pick the strings and sing.
There are torches everywhere, there are faces
swimming in shine and sweat and beer and grins and greed.
There are tapers confusing the stacked spears.
There are queens on their knees at idols, crosses, lamps.
There are handstand clowns knocked headlong by maudlin heroes.
There are candles in the sleazy bowers, the whores
sleep all day with mice across their feet.
The slung warhorn gleams in the drizzle,
the horses shift their hooves and shiver.
It is all a pestilence, life within life
and movement within movement, lips meeting,
grooming of mares, roofs plated with gold,
hunted pelts laid on kings,
neck-veins bursting from greasy torques,
pouches of coins gamed off, slaves and outlaws
eating hailstones under heaven.
Who would be a man? Who would be the winter sparrow
that flies at night by mistake into a lighted hall
and flutters the length of it in zigzag panic,
dazed and terrified by the heat and noise and smoke,
the drink-fumes and the oaths, the guttering flames,
feast-bones thrown to a snarl of wolfhounds,
flash of swords in sodden sorry quarrels,
till at last he sees the other door
and skims out in relief and joy
into the stormy dark?
— Black grove, black lake, black sky,
no shoe or keel or wing undoes your stillness
as I plod through the fens and prowl
in my own place and sometimes stand many hours, as now,
above those unreflecting waters, reflecting as I can
on men, and on their hideous clamorous brilliance
that beats the ravens' beaks into the ground
and douses a million funeral pyres.

Jack London in Heaven

Part the clouds, let me look down.
Oh god that earth. A breeze comes from the sea
and humpback fogs blanch off to blindness, the sun
hits Frisco, it shines solid up to heaven.
I can't bear not to see a brisk day on the Bay,
it drives me out of my mind but I can't bear
not to watch the choppy waters, Israfel.
I got a sea-eagle once to come up here
screaming and turn a prayer-wheel or two
with angry buffets till the sharpshooters
sent him to hell, and I groaned,
grew dark with disfavour. — What,
I should pray now? For these thoughts?
Here are some more. I was up at four
for psalms, shawms, smarms, salaams, yessirs, yesmaams,
felt-tipped hosannas melting into mist,
a mushroom high, an elation of vapours,
a downpour of dumpy amens. Azazel,
I am sick of fireflies. It's a dumb joss.
— You know I'm a spoilt angel? What happens to us?
I'm not so bright — or bright, perhaps. God knows!
They almost let me fall through heaven craning
to see sunshine dappling the heaving gunmetal
of the Oakland Estuary — the crawl, the swell, the crests
I could pull up to touch and wet my hands
let down a moment into time and space.
How long will they allow me to remember
as I pick the cloud-rack apart and peer?
The estuary, Israfel, the glittery estuary, August '96!
My last examination has scratched to a finish,
I'm rushing to the door, whooping and squawking,
I dance down the steps, throw my hat in the air
as the dusty invigilator frowns, gathers in
that furious harvest of four months' cramming,
nineteen hours a day — my vigils, Azazel,
my holy vigils — the oyster-pirate hammering

at the gates of the state university.
It's enough. I got in. But at that time
I took a boat out on the ebb
to be alone where no book ever was.
I scudded dreaming through the creamy rings
of light and water, followed the shore
and thought of earth and heaven and myself
till I saw a shipyard I knew, and the delta rushes
and the weeds and the tin wharves, and smelt the ropes
and some tobacco-smoke, and longed for company.
— Evensong? I'm not coming to evensong.
Get off, get away. Go on, sing for your supper!
Bloody angels! — So I sailed in, made fast,
and there was Charley, and Liz, and Billy and Joe, and Dutch
— that desperate handsome godlike drunken man —
old friends, Azazel, old friends that clambered over me
and sang and wept and filled me with whisky and beer
brought teetering across the railroad tracks
all that long noon.
They would have kept me there, oh, for ever
but I could see the blue through the open door,
that blue, my sea, and they knew
I had to be away, and got me stumbling down the wharf steps
into a good salmon boat, with charcoal and a brazier
and coffee and a pot and a pan and a fresh-caught fish
and cast me off into a stiff wind.
I tell you, Israfel, the sea was white
and half of it was in my boat
with my sail set hard like a board.
Everything whipped and cracked
in pure green glory as
I stood braced at the mast
and roared out 'Shenandoah'.
Did Odysseus get to heaven?
I came down to earth, at Antioch,
sobered in the sunset shadows, tied up
alongside a potato sloop, had friends
aboard there too, who sizzled my fish for me

and gave me stew and crusty bread and claret,
claret in great pint mugs, and wrapped me in blankets
warmer and softer than the clouds of heaven.
What did we not talk of as we smoked,
sea-tales Odysseus might have known,
under the same night wind, the same wild rigging.
— Azazel, I must get down there!
I am a wasting shade, I am drifting and dying
by these creeping streams. If you are my friend,
tell them my trouble. Tell them
they cannot make me a heaven
like the tide-race and the tiller
and a broken-nailed hand
and the shrouds of Frisco.

Cinquevalli

Cinquevalli is falling, falling.
The shining trapeze kicks and flirts free,
solo performer at last.
The sawdust puffs up with a thump,
settles on a tangle of broken limbs.
St Petersburg screams and leans.
His pulse flickers with the gas-jets. He lives.

Cinquevalli has a therapy.
In his hospital bed, in his hospital chair
he holds a ball, lightly, lets it roll round his hand,
or grips it tight, gauging its weight and resistance,
begins to balance it, to feel its life attached to his
by will and knowledge, invisible strings
that only he can see. He throws it
from hand to hand, always different,
always the same, always
different, always the

same.
His muscles learn to think, his arms grow very strong.

Cinquevalli in sepia
looks at me from an old postcard: bundle of enigmas.
Half faun, half military man; almond eyes, curly hair,
conventional moustache; tights, and a tunic loaded
with embroideries, tassels, chains, fringes; hand on hip
with a large signet-ring winking at the camera
but a bull neck and shoulders and a cannon-ball
at his elbow as he stands by the posing pedestal;
half reluctant, half truculent,
half handsome, half absurd,
but let me see you forget him: not to be done.

Cinquevalli is a juggler.
In a thousand theatres, in every continent,
he is the best, the greatest. After eight years perfecting
he can balance one billiard ball on another billiard ball
on top of a cue on top of a third billiard ball
in a wine-glass held in his mouth. To those
who say the balls are waxed, or flattened,
he patiently explains the trick will only work
because the spheres are absolutely true.
There is no deception in him. He is true.

Cinquevalli is juggling with a bowler,
a walking-stick, a cigar, and a coin.
Who foresees? How to please.
The last time round, the bowler
flies to his head, the stick sticks in his hand,
the cigar jumps into his mouth, the coin
lands on his foot — ah, but
is kicked into his eye
and held there as the miraculous monocle
without which the portrait would be incomplete.

Cinquevalli is practising.
He sits in his dressing-room talking to some friends,
at the same time writing a letter with one hand
and with the other juggling four balls.
His friends think of demons, but
"You could do all this," he says,
sealing the letter with a billiard ball.

Cinquevalli is on the high wire in Odessa.
The roof cracks, he is falling, falling
into the audience, a woman breaks his fall,
he cracks her like a flea, but lives.

Cinquevalli broods in his armchair in Brixton Road.
He reads in the paper about the shells whining
at Passchendaele, imagines the mud and the dead.
He goes to the window and wonders through that dark evening
what is happening in Poland where he was born.
His neighbours call him a German spy.
"Kestner, Paul Kestner, that's his name!"
"Keep Kestner out of the British music-hall!"
He frowns; it is cold; his fingers seem stiff and old.

Cinquevalli tosses up a plate of soup
and twirls it on his forefinger; not a drop spills.
He laughs, and well may he laugh
who can do that. The astonished table
breathe again, laugh too, think the world
a spinning thing that spills, for a moment, no drop.

Cinquevalli's coffin sways through Brixton
only a few months before the Armistice.
Like some trick they cannot get off the ground
it seems to burden the shuffling bearers, all their arms
cross-juggle that displaced person, that man
of balance, of strength, of delights and marvels,
in his unsteady box at last into the earth.

Resistance

The fog rolled through the valley in great force.
The bridge was down, they'd never leave that night.
Once the girl got sticks and made a fire
it was quite snug. McAndrew had his flask.
The old organ took Curly's arpeggios
very decently, and there was trout for supper.
Poor Black thought he heard gunfire, but
he was always hearing things. Owls, yes,
but any guns were in the next valley. Niven
brushed out her hair with her back to the fire
as if she'd always lived there. No one lived there
except the dotty caretaker, and he'd gone
to bed. Rod was telling stories about fog
in that ursa major voice of his, when
Black said "Listen!" and there were four smart taps
on the french window. The girl swore afterwards
she'd seen a shape, but it was only fog —
the snow would have left footprints. Branches?
Nothing was near. Bats then? Scrabbling
was not the sound, it was knuckles on glass.
"I tell you —" Black began, but the macabre
is of limited interest, like far-off gunfire,
and this is not a ghost story. Curly thought
the glass was cracking in unaccustomed heat
from the fire; Rod said it was the organ.
They laughed, and wrestled on the sheepskin.
At first light they all left for the next valley,
blowing on their hands. "Snowshoes!" the girl cried,
but there was no one listening, in that wind.
So they found out nothing of the stranger
who tapped the glass at dark and disappeared.
They missed the code. They walked right into it.

Heaven

We have seen too many films
to be bowled over by many mansions,
but still, there it was: big, mostly bright,
crowding off as far as the eye could see,
a palimpsest of saved burrows and pinnacles
in so many dimensions it seemed insubstantial,
yet busy with colour, smells, cries, stripes of light
like an old bazaar.
Bizarre! And keys at the gate! Incredible! Rings of them,
ancient, made of metal, for each arriver —
and no instructions to find your own place.
We have had too many nightmares
not to know that winding drive
that grows darker and darker
overhung with rhododendrons.
Shaking, we follow it
to the black, mossed porch.
The house is derelict.
We tiptoe up the stair
to the last room
with the last key
and get it to growl
round in its hole
and let us push into
paradise, paradise
please, if we may.

Story

The leaves are stills of sky, glow
unblown. The engine
ticking over where we've stopped
shocks out the glen grasshoppers.

The Cuillins cut out of violet velvet
waver through the road heat ahead.
The shouts of climbers when I switch off
come clear across their distance.
The thermos pours its startled tea
loud as a waterfall. The steam
winds past your eyes
which watch me. The
seventh sentence is not yet translated
from the original.

Remora

Hungry I am, but I feed
on following, I never feed
on the great chair of command
and ask my thousands to bring platters, I bend
my neck and wait on my lord.
Parasites fees on parasites and
I believe I am in a middling sort of grind.
The great one cannot shake me off, and in the end
if he is sick, or failing, I find
another great one and I bind
my little demand
into his broad-backed slaughterhouse of blood.

French

It is like leafing through a book of hours,
these slow hot days, each gilded,
each green and blue, each crisp and fragile with
the flames a possible next page. Madame

de Vionnet spreads her parasol, the shadow
flutters on the creamy river, her lover
sits on his jacket, rows towards the twilight.
He would row on for ever, with no guilt
that was not like the stripes and gutterings
of shade the brilliant water fends off from
boat and arm and oar. But hell is near:
they are seen. The devils sing; the veils
of Madame de Vionnet cage her rouge, her age.
He swears, and jettisons his cigarette.
She is worth the gesture and the spark. Pas davantage.

Testament

Through the storm he walked before he gave his sermon.
The sails were whipped to shreds. He took a turn.
There was hardly any air not dense with spray,
they choked as they half saw him out there
going or coming, who knows, through the sea-lumps.
His face was like a sheet of lightning. "Beside him,
his injured arm in a sling, was Red Nelson,
his sou'wester gone and his fair hair plastered in wet,
wind-blown ringlets about his face. His whole attitude
breathed indomitability, courage, strength.
It seemed almost as though the divine
were blazing forth from him." They shipped water,
baled, shipped water, baled, baled, baled.
Things blew themselves out. They tottered to shore,
too busy to see him back on board,
though he'd baled, he told them. There was no sermon.
They dried their rags on stones, he kept his on,
sitting a little apart, his sou'wester gone
and his fair hair plastered in wet, wind-blown
ringlets about his face. His whole attitude breathed
indomitability, courage, strength. It seemed
almost as though the divine were blazing forth from him.

They asked me to write this faithfully.
I do, and yet I am not sure that I do.
Sometimes I frown at what the pen has said.
My understanding breaks in waves, dissolves.
I am tired of walking on the sea.
Give me ice or vapour, terra firma,
some change that is a change not a betrayal.
Water would be water even with footprints
soldered to it in characters of fire
— as they were that day — God knows — as they were!

Night Pillion

Eleven struck. The traffic lights were green.
The shuddering machine let out its roar
As we sprang forward into brilliant streets.
Beyond your shoulders and helmet the walls rose
Well into darkness, mounted up, plunged past —
Hunting the clouds that hunted the few stars.
And now the neons thinned, the moon was huge.
The gloomy river lay in a glory, the bridge
In its mists as we rode over it slowly sighed.
We lost the shining tram-lines in the slums
As we kept south; the shining trolley-wires
Glinted through Gorbals; on your helmet a glint hung.
A cat in a crumbling close-mouth, a lighted window
With its shadow-play, a newspaper in the wind —
The night swept them up even as we slowed,
Our wheels jolting over the buckled causeys.
But my net swept up night and cat and road
And mine is the shadow-play that window showed
And mine the paper with its cries and creases.
— Shadow-play? What we flashed past was life
As what we flash into is life, and life
Will not stand still until within one flash

Of words or paint or human love it stops
Transfixed, and drops its pain and grime
Into forgetful time.
But I remember: I saw the flash: and then
We met the moonlit Clyde again, swung off
And roared in a straight run for Rutherglen.
The wind whistled by the football ground
And by the waste ground that the seagulls found.
The long wail of a train recalled the city
We had left behind, and mingled with the wind.
Whatever it was that sang in me there
As we neared home, I give it no name here.
But tenements and lives, the wind, our wheels,
The vibrant windshield and your guiding hands
Fell into meaning, whatever meaning it was —
Whatever joy it was —
And my blood quickened in me as I saw
Everything guided, vibrant, where our shadow
Glided along the pavements and the walls.
Perhaps I only saw the thoroughfares,
The river, the dancing of the foundry-flares?
Joy is where long solitude dissolves.
I rode with you towards human needs and cares.

from *The Dictionary of Tea*

tea top: a musical, spinning samovar.

the Tea Theatre: the highest theatre in the world; home of the
    Darjeeling Drama.

tea hod: small hod for carrying tea bricks in Tibet.

tea square: an impotent Dervish.

tea cloud: a high calm soft warm light gold cloud, sometimes seen at sunset.

teafish: bred by the Japanese in special fish-farms, where it feeds on tannin-impregnated potato extract, this famous fish is the source of our 'instant fish teas', tasting equally of fish, chips, and tea.

tea cat: species of giant toad found in South India; it is not a cat, and has no connection with tea.

grey tea: used of a disappointment. E.g. "Harriet got her grey tea that night."

brown bolus tea: an old-fashioned medicine, of which the true recipe has been lost.

tea stays: so called, in Edwardian times, because they added elegance to the gestures of a hostess pouring tea.

sea tea: sailors' term for plankton bouillon.

Cook in Hawaii

The English gods have outstayed their welcome.
They have stripped the island of tribute —
coconuts, breadfruit, pigs and plantains, water.
They have come limping back from a gale
with a broken mast for repair.
They have anchored again and splashed ashore,
commanded a hunt for the sailmakers.
Hawaiians mutter, gather on the beach.
You won't take that king hostage, Captain Cook!
The queen shrieks, cries, prays, tugs, entreats
her people. The people ring the captain round. The captain

leaves the king, retreats. He's grim, his feet
are on the beach. Hawaiians shout
and jostle him. The blue sky's pure, a swallow's there.
The human error builds. That island
you won't leave now, Captain Cook! —
won't leave living, won't leave whole.
Is there to be no understanding at all?
At the shallow-water rocks he stands
and gestures to the launch. His back
is to the islanders, Captain Fool, Captain Fool!
His back is full of daggers
and he's face down in the shallows
threshing faintly with his feet,
Captain Cook. The blood gushes, rushes, races
to discover the Pacific.

The Break-In

I took a mop and swabbed the burglar's blood
from windows, walls, and floor. The spray and trail
of arteries punctured by the shards of panes
he had himself broken, entering, and was broken on,
leaving, spread down three stairs and made the block
of flats a Hitchcock set, but real, so real
that as I knelt when my mop refused the stains,
and had to rub a grey rag into them
and get, through two cuts on my fingers, his
blood into mine, not knowing yet he was
a hepatitis-ridden addict, I
re-lived that cursing stagger step by step,
and spot by spot tried to but could not blot
the dark blood from my mind. A buttock jab
takes care of hepatitis; record-player,
radio, watch, cheque-book, kitchen purse
are mortal goods that come and go. Not there

the invasion, the invisible assault,
as landings forget neighbours' running feet,
and shocked rooms spring back slowly into place,
and walkie-talkies fade along the road,
and the uneasiest of sullen nights
comes down and wraps things in an aspirin throb
of memories and apprehensiveness:
the greater break-in was not through those walls
but into my reddened hands, into my blood.

An Alphabet of Goddesses

Aphrodite

She tramps in long tight boots like a hussar.
Her girdle is a brace of promises.
The sea-foam has long left her and she brims
blinding out of crimson velvet and smoky mink
and she shakes like a tumbril, shocked and shocking
chockfull of longing but not forlorn,
red captain wrinkling on her gloves,
black captain flashing her epaulettes,
silver captain slipping her stole,
headless captain with flesh like lightning.
Her marathon is the coast of desire,
vast melon-slice of sugar and ginger.
She strides and strikes through the flushy strands!
She cannot know who follows her, kingfisher, queenfisher!
She cuts out thought, the love of gods and men.

Bacche

The hot slopes buzzed with honey,
the caves dripped with hives.
She swore the air livid over all Libya
as she set the honey-pot and the acorns and the mash of roots

at the feet of her skittish changeling,
her flop-eared half-horned stinking growing
goat-thing, her filthy four-legged foster-child,
her god-willed, god-wild
charge
and care.
Her nails were in shreds with digging the earth,
her black hair hung in dusty knots.
She raged down into Africa
for a child to give honey to,
and gave all gods to Gehenna,
and the goat-god to the pits below Gehenna
even as she fed him
from her commanded hand.

Circe

She thought she could live on the capital of weather-hard
    Odysseus
having stacked his shield and spear at her door
and scampered in her bed that long time,
but now she has grown old there seem to be
no sunny days on her alder-dark island,
no fleets of sailors to entice ashore,
nothing but to chatter to herself by the stove.
What should a scrawny black marmoset
hold up her breasts to — men, mirrors, thunder?
She has got rid of all her mirrors,
and her best men are hogs that root among the thickets,
no longer able to rise on their hind-legs
and snout her with all they remembered of a kiss.
She remembers much, but it is going.
Her scrag-tail droops, her spells falter.
— Then she pulls on her black stockings, right up,
and screeches as she scrapes a nail
along the nylon like a welder's spark,
and pins on her old sphinx headdress from Cairo
with its mortal colours, immortal desires.

Demeter

When her daughter was taken she was distracted,
set fire to the silos, drowned cornfields in paraquat.
Travelling folk saw her looming blowsily
with her chainsaw among the oaks.
Her temples pounded, she was brown as the earth.
She cursed the burrs that clung to her back,
swore at the rolling fields. In her fury she was a queen.
The blood of many gods was stirred. She saw them
from the corner of her eye, their hands on their buckles,
their glances on her tatters. She changed herself
into a mare and watched them melt beyond the trees.
But she forgot there were gods too in the seas.
Poseidon laughed and splashed up like an octopus
and made himself into a hippopotamus
(too large) and a sea-horse (too tiny) and lastly
into a horse that met the case, and quickly
cantered through the marram-grass and covered her.
"It is not every day —" she mused
and nicely showed her teeth.

Eileithyia

Who is greater than Eileithyia?
Crossing, uncrossing her knees
in Chaos she brought Heaven
Earth and Love to birth.
Leviathan swims in her lap;
she snaps pods of men
and gods. Goddesses, women
cry to her; mare,
vixen, doe, ewe
lean into her back
once that hour strikes.
Childbearers, shieldbearers:
standing in their husbands' arms
in a quiet room, swaying
in water for the baby to pop

125

to the surface like a fish, crouching
in the foul rubble of a shelled
city with shudders too early,
caught without a telephone
in a rush of blood, they wait
on the mother of gods and men.
Run, Eileithyia, from the ends
of the earth. Terrible, be kind!

Fortuna

You want to keep your man? You want to catch your boy?
You want a raunchy bed? You want to give good head?
> She needs a little prayer,
> she doesn't ask a lot
> but better late than not.

You wish you were a geisha, with tea and tease and teeter?
You're set to be a stripper? Have champers in a slipper?
> She needs a little payment,
> she doesn't ask a lot
> but better late than not.

You must have two-way mirrors and a cache of bootleg videos?
You'd like a good address-book, a handy line in widowers?
> She needs a little patience,
> she doesn't ask a lot
> but better late than not.

And when you've got your gigolo, your gold taps, your jacuzzi O,
And are snug as a bug in your circular bed, with pots of caviar
    black and red,
> She needs some little praises,
> she doesn't ask a lot
> but safer late than not.

Gaea

When the earth had barely stopped being wild,
and the continents were grumbling down onto their day-beds,
the earth-mother could not contain herself
with the thought of life. She made the sky
give lightning, bluster, bruise, press, drench.
She had a fire cave. She whistled.
She ground the sea in a pot.
She hardly felt the monsters leave her
that were born to grieve her; guffawed
when she saw the first belly-knot,
but smiled at the second,
checked the third was there,
never noticed the fourth,
grew angry with the fifth.
A dozen roaring clumsy plated titans
scorned her dandling; towering one-eyed loners
roamed off, raised cyclopean forts; like walking redwoods,
hundred-handed giants flailed the groves.
What was she feeling for in her gross, careless prime?
Not giant times,
not beauty then,
not goodness yet,
but women, men.

Hecate

She does not love you. She is not good luck.
If there are forces of evil, she is high in their councils.
She does not like this world, but will use it.
She has made so much magic she has no shape.
Sometimes she has a dog's head and feeds on the dead.
Sometimes she is only your shadow, maybe.
What is pleasant to her, apart from slow limousines?
Gin; acid; bugles; and the moon shining on these.

Ismene

"Forgive me, Antigone my sister, I did not think
you were right to be so bold, and the tyrant so strong.
Now I see that even if you die
he has met his match in you, and I draw strength
from your strength and I mean to share your fate.
I thought of our poor brother's body naked exposed
to wandering dogs and carrion birds, in my mind
I was with you and helped you scatter dust.
It is not too late to tend a shoot of courage!
There is a desert where they will take us
and they will wall us slowly into a cave
— oh sister, hold me, hold me Antigone! —
and empty a wineskin before the last brick
while we try not to scream at the white sun
and suddenly the workman's brow and eyes
steady serious detached appraising
will fill the measured gap and at once
the brick will be scraped out and tapped into the dark
and I shall not cry out or faint but put
my head on your shoulder, sister, if I may,
in that tomb."

Jocasta

She had guessed long ago   but gave up the thought
as too grubby, too godless.   The green in his eye
had a family strangeness?   That failed to stick.
There were gaps in his story,   but so it goes.
Coincidence rules   in cradles not royal
as on couches in Corinth.   Kings command,
gods garble.   Pieces slip from the game.
Some said in malice   she might have been his mother,
but bitching throve   in bored Thebes.
She married him, cherished him,   gave him four children.
The great bedroom was blue   and blazing with gold.
Rain rang on the roof;   white sheets rustled.
When the sun was near   he would stretch naked,

fall on her at cockcrow   with uncooled force.
Yet his mate was his mother,   as mouths had breathed
and as she had half known   yet needed him the more.
When everything was revealed   she veiled herself, vomited,
ran with a rough rope   under the rafters
and swung in purple   to be purged of her son.

Kore

In her forearms the faint
creak of wet hyacinths
as she ran across the field
brushed and diffused
a fresh, half-sick
pungent fragrance
that followed her, though
she would never touch
the tight sexy curls.
Spring became summer,
late brooding summer;
in the heat and heaviness
she let her flushed cheek
cool itself on petals
of a blood-red rose.
She would make love
to the very trees
when they turn yellow
and chestnuts thud
into the beech-mast.
She is bound for the underworld
and the creaking bed
of grim, strong, aged
pitiless Hades,
Through his cold thrust
wish her well.

Lethe

She has been lobotomized with Naomi Ginsberg but she does
not forget.
She has been stoned in Khomeini's brickyard but she does not
forget.
She has hung in a cage at Cumae wasting away but she does not
forget.
She has burned in Israeli phosphorus for hours but she does not
forget.
She has crackled in the market-place at Rouen but she does not
forget.
She has been injected with kerosine in Belsen but she does not
forget.
She has drunk the lees of Chappaquiddick but she does not
forget.

> There is nothing you can pay her for the waters
> of oblivion. High in a glittering sieve
> she holds them, pans for grains of mercy.
> There is no ferry, no other life.
> Hunger and thirst after righteousness.

Medea

Snake-charmer, illusionist, aeronaut, chemist, chameleon,
multiple murderess; she had death and love
struggling under her black cowl like maimed eagles.
We are told that when she first saw pirate Jason
shaking his rings and squinting up into the sun
she got a superhuman shot from sardonic Eros —
the arrow blasted into her right to the feathers.
And when Jason left her for Creusa,
she put on a pleasant mask and ran up a little white dress
which she sent as a wedding-gift, and when Creusa
had stepped into it and her maid zipped it up tight
it was like striking a match: up she went
in flames, and it stuck to her like napalm
as she ran through the palace, setting fire to others
in a chain of charred vengeance.

130

And she who had dismembered her own brother for Jason,
and for Jason had seethed his usurping uncle in a cauldron,
now made a sacrifice of the two sons Jason had given her —
the altar's crimson shouted her dry eyes.
And she pulled on her hood, and wrote in her diary:
"I am not accountable. Gods are not grocers.
The arrow is in my side. I got the golden fleece."

Nemesis

She will have you on a plate with two forks.
She knows the bad apple in the barrel.
She is the crab that comes at you the wrong way.
Her teeth grind exceeding small.
She controls the roulette-wheel — but don't bet on it.
She holds the ladder for you, and kicks it away.
Don't cry, How tragic! She loves comedy.
Don't laugh your head off; she might keep it.
One thing, though: never try to deceive her.
Propitiation is her *bête noire*.
But you must hold yourself in readiness,
and put your advisers on a slow train.

Oreithyia

In the beginning she swirled up naked
out of Chaos, before anything was made.
Out of Chaos she made a sort of wild sea and
over it and on it she skimmed and splashed with delight.
Over it and her she pegged up a sky:
it was blue, grey, black, as wild as the sea, and
it was to ward off infinity.
It was then between the sea and the sky she felt
almost at home, though alone,
almost able to dance, and she did dance
all the more wildly in her loneliness,
all the more intently in that wildness.
Arms flew, hair flew, breasts flew,
a vortex for Boreas. And the north wind rushed on her,

eagerly entered her, endlessly
impregnates her, plays with her, presses her, dances with her
in wildness and in order,
in order to make earth and stars,
animals and people
and everything that can be made.
Auroras dance over them; they mate for
aeons. And swelling, gorgeous, bloody, a
universe kicks
itself out.

Pasiphae

"Why should Aphrodite keep us down,
trudging about as servants in our dim robes,
testing her wine for poison, tracking her lost veils,
traipsing for rouge, combs, fans, roses, toothpicks?
the three Graces are the three Stupid Ones, sisters!"
— So she tore off her moth-brown jellaba,
and put on a topless feathery wool tunic
and strutted like a Sumerian temple harlot,
and then she spread out her arms and made them into wings,
flapped them and danced in quick angry swoops
until her feet became claws and as a bird
she could scold at Aphrodite and cast a shadow over her.
But Aphrodite plunged in the palace pool like a seal
and came up sleek glittering august invulnerable unmatchable
while jealous Pasiphae stood and screamed like a peacock,
and scuttered among the garden herms with her desperate lament,
sawing the impotent air.

Queen Alcyone

Halcyon days are calm and strong.
She hears and loves the sailors' song.

She watches for the sudden storm
and guards her captains free from harm.

She sees the snake-like waterspout
and shares the rowers' trembling shout.

She raises up her great winged head,
interposing dread for dread

until tornadoes hiss and turn
and sails regain the timid sun.

Sometimes her wings are blue in blue
as sea and sky melt in and through

her brooding stillness to a scene
unimaginably serene

where hurricanes have never been
and Alcyone is queen.

But mostly men must grip the rail
and hope they will not roar or quail

when crashing lumps and darkness rise
to pound and drown one more poor prize.

Rhea

"What was it like while you were a snake?"
"You mean when he was a snake too?" "Who, Zeus?"
"Zeus, who else! Well, it was different.
It was certainly slitherier, if you like that;
very close, since nothing gets in the way.
I thought I would never go back to crude hugs
the first time I felt the slow travelling ripple:
it catches every inch of you in its squeeze
but in succession, severally, subtly, not
with one blunt anthropomorphic gasp
as four limbs fall on you dumped on a bed."
"But — ?" "But, yes, well, it palls.

You don't really seem to get any nearer.
What it lacks is purchase, resistance."
"Can't you anchor your tails — a tree, a rock?"
"No, we tried, but there was no grip.
You don't exactly have a tail, you are all tail."
"He made it, though?" "Oh yes, after a deal
of threshing and twisting about, he made it."
"Your son." "What do you mean my son?"
"Zeus is your own son." "Zeus was a snake
and I was a snake. *That* never came
out of my womb. Use your imagination."
"I wish I had seen it. He must have coursed you
like a spaceship, you are both such titans.
You must have tangled like arms of nebulas,
or two galaxies passing through each other,
signals for some millennial dish."
"I'm a goddess again. Make me a wish."

Sphinx

What has the head and breasts of a woman and the hungry body
of a lioness and the wings of a bird of prey and the long tail of
a snake lashing slowly from side to side as it lies crouched on
the branch of a tree on a busy boulevard and keeps asking
pedestrians what is the square root of minus one and what
was the song the sirens sang and why is it easier for a rich
man to ride his camel into heaven than for three million
unemployed to pass through the eye of a needle and how
long would it take for the genetic mutations following an
all-out nuclear attack to produce a creature with the head
and breasts of a woman and the hungry body of a lioness
and the wings of a bird of prey and the long tail of a snake
lashing slowly from side to side as it lies crouched on the
branch of a tree on a busy boulevard asking pedestrians
endless questions and when they cannot answer swings
round its huge hungry lion-haunches and strangles them
with its sphincter?

I give up.

Terpsichore

She has made a jukebox video and is really jumping.
Her image flickers in the wired-up lay-bys,
gives you a charge in airport concourse bars.
In the twenty-first century AD/BC AC/DC she
is a body-stocking of poetry and pleasure, a kick
of fervent music in very very dark red,
with gloves, studs, belt of rarest Ravenscraig steel
and a lacquered helmet blond as corn.
She is not programmed, but she has a programme,
and that is to dance heaven down into your arms
with showers of gold direct
or alternating, rippling
like the wind.
And she will dance to heaven and you,
and you to her, and heaven to the two;
behind you soft mock-Tiffany lamps,
in front of you the whole laser-show,
and a gantry scarlet with hyperlager,
and a well-sprung floor and a welter of decibels,
the waves and shouts of day-glo nights,
the waves and shouts of day-glo nights.
— With what slow pain she will then draw it all back,
scarcely moving, drifting like a mime,
putting a finger to your lips,
binding the feet of heaven.
The paraphernalia roll off like tumbleweed.
Cameramen hold their ground. She looks at them.
They make her most beautiful video
of dawn, and the dying dance.

Urania

There was a raven on Mount Ararat
who came when he was called; she pampered him.
She also loved to watch the choughs that skim
these highest terraces; even a bat
would take her fancy. For it was all flight,

flight, flight! The white observatory dome
opened and shut as if it was her home,
but she was out there, in eternal night!
Her headdress was a comet, and the sands
of Mars were sown into her streaming robes.
Astronomy is not for hausfrau hearts!
Her signals travelled on a million bands,
and when she launched her own Olympian probes
it was to star and brim the starless charts.

Vixen

The Vixen of Teumessus, red-haired rager,
sniffs and barks and yelps for youths.
She is stronger than any trap.
Her sleeves never snag on brambles
as she runs through the woods
where young men saunter.
She marks her victim where he leans on a tree.
With a growl she pinions him, ties him to the trunk,
bares her breast, takes out her whip,
lashes him carefully, slowly, painfully,
loosens her skirt, draws his blood steadily,
moans with him, lets her long tongue dangle,
excites him with her rank hot breath,
lashes him quickly, sharply, deeply,
till at last with a cry he jerks at the ropes,
stains the ground red and white together.
> "And so he will release," she said,
> "the lushest groves in Greece," she said.
>> But nothing more grew there
>> than came from rain and air.
>>> So she was overthrown
>>> and turned to stone.

Wisdom

Wisdom-Titaness Metis, first wife of Zeus,
sitting motionless massive unsmiling in her grey tunic,
her pale feet on a cloud shaped like a globe,

her arms at rest in her lap, her eyes unblinking,
will suddenly be on her feet, in profile, kicking
the cloud down limbo, staring at a new thought,
her robe gone black, or white, a hand at her ear
to cup and amplify the faint spidery grating
of a nebula's arm as it goes akimbo in Cygnus,
and as suddenly again dive down silently
into the watery universe like a ziggurat in Atlantis.
Does she know everything? What she knows, she knows.
Does she know everything? She is a time queen;
millionaires with trembling piggy-banks
mean nothing to her, she does not sell.
Does she know everything? She is a woman
and she knows gross bold Jove waits at her side
to cut her exponential empire,
to divorce her troubling wisdom,
to devour her threatening knowledge,
but she does not know when.
She spreads her arms along the back of her throne.

Xenaea

She said if she saw him still two-timing her
she would make sure he never saw again.
He was tired of her tantrums and told her so.

When she watched how he settled the woman into her cloak
at the end of the next party, she knew they were lovers,
even if their obvious happiness had not told her so.

She said nothing, but went into her kitchen
when the servants were absent, and picked out a strong skewer
which she found she could conceal in the sleeve of her dress.

At their next meeting he seemed vaguely contrite,
brought her some pretty violets, but it was too late.
She had hardened her heart, and when he sat beside her

she rose quickly and without saying a single word
plunged the skewer into his eyes in turn.
It was only at his pitiful screams she began to shake,

and in the pain of love blinded herself,
standing in front of the grandest of bronze mirrors
any goddess ever held up to grief.

Youth

Trays and pitchers, glasses, flagons at the high table!
Cupbearer Hebe, youth-goddess, happy, all grace!
Flash of her white napkins, clack of her quick sandals!
The torches flickered, her shadow painted the floor.

The torches flicker, her shadow paints the floor.
White staring stiff and cold she is carried
into the deadly fields, takes no drink and gives none.
Her merry heart is only memory.

Her merry heart will be the memory
of youth that passes, and if it could last
would lose its happiness. Pitchers pour
without stint when they make us say they do,

in glasses on the changing changeless table.

Zeuxippe

Hyperborean ponies
followed her; she could not have enough of them.
She had sugar for a troop.
"Hey!" and "Whoa!" and "Holaho!" she would cry
as she scoured the stubble
or stood on knowes and mounds
and counted manes.
She had no care for power,
had long left palaces, been written off,

her name almost forgotten.
But when she sniffed the north wind
she knew her own country,
and ran with her horses along the broken strand,
the wild gusts blowing off to the horizon
her "Hey!" and "Whoa!" and "Holaho!".